Joseph Jacobs

George Eliot, Matthew Arnold, Browning, Newman

Essays and Reviews from the 'Athenaeum'

Joseph Jacobs

George Eliot, Matthew Arnold, Browning, Newman
Essays and Reviews from the 'Athenaeum'

ISBN/EAN: 9783337138929

Printed in Europe, USA, Canada, Australia, Japan

Cover: Foto ©Thomas Meinert / pixelio.de

More available books at **www.hansebooks.com**

GEORGE ELIOT
MATTHEW ARNOLD
BROWNING
NEWMAN

ESSAYS AND REVIEWS

FROM THE 'ATHENÆUM'

BY

JOSEPH JACOBS

Shall we say: 'Let the ages judge the spirits!' Why, we are the beginning of the ages.

GEORGE ELIOT

LONDON
Published by DAVID NUTT
in the Strand
1891

PREFACE

I have explained in the Introduction why I have thought it worth while to reprint these 'éloges' of four of the chief English writers who died in the last decade and to add certain reviews of books by or about them. I desire here to emphasise the fact that these obituaries were in every case written within the two or three days that elapsed between the death of their subjects and the appearance of the ensuing issue of the 'Athenæum.' I have nothing to say against the practice of others, but I cannot myself anticipate the Great Destroyer.

I have to thank the Publisher and Editor of the 'Athenæum' for their kind and ready permission to reprint these articles from its pages.

J. J.

CONTENTS

The date after each entry refers to the Number of the *Athenæum* in which the article appeared.

INTRODUCTION

THE first few days after a great writer's death are critical for his reputation. Then for the first time we realise all that he has been to us, all that he has done for us. We can for the first time speak of his whole work with little fear of the surprises that genius has often in store for the critic who dares to be prophetic. We can speak out our full thought of him, if for no other reason, because what we say cannot by any chance come before him. Above all, he has ceased to be a person, and we can treat more simply and directly of his spiritual influence. At the same time we that speak are those who have come under his spell in his lifetime and express the feelings of his contemporaries without any of the disturbing influences which later revelations or the modification of the *Zeitgeist* produce on the appeal he may have for after-times. We alone can say what he has been to us whom he addressed.

It has chanced during the past ten years that I have been called upon to give on behalf of the

Athenæum an estimate of the loss English Letters have sustained by the death of the four chief writers who left us during the decade. These essays differed, I believe, in at least two respects from the obituary notices which swarm from the press on such occasions. They were estimates, not obituaries; they dealt rather with the work than with the life of each author. And they were written immediately on hearing of the death of the writer concerned, whereas it is well known that every newspaper has obituaries of all the notabilities of the time pigeon-holed for production on the morrow of the death. Whatever then the merits of these essays, they were written under the influence of the feelings I have indicated above, and were in each case, I may perhaps say, the first critical estimate of contemporary England on the lifework of these great writers. That they appeared in the foremost literary journal of the English-speaking peoples gives them an importance that I could not claim for any personal utterances. I have for these reasons thought them worthy of being put in more permanent form as documents—'documents' is a favourite word and thing just now—in the history of English opinion about the writers treated in this volume. At the same time I have thought it right to leave them in substantially the same form as that in which they first appeared, only removing a few traces of necessarily hasty writing. 'Documents' must not be falsified. I may perhaps venture to add, in fairness to myself, that there are some few things in them which I would have put differently if I had been writing over my own name in the first instance.

To make this little volume more worthy of acceptance, I have added a few reviews of works written by or about the authors treated. These also appeared in the *Athenæum* for the most part after the death of the subjects of my *éloges*. They were more detailed estimates of parts of the authors' works, or they dealt more at large with their lives, or in other ways they seemed to me to supplement the more general *éloges* written for a special occasion from a special point of view.

Looking back on these memorial essays, I can now discern the general method on which they were formed, though I was not conscious of it at the time of writing. At the moment of an author's death, we think primarily of the man we have lost. But we mourn the man for the sake of his works, hence it is those of his qualities that are shown in his works which naturally engage our attention at the moment of his death. These essays are therefore appropriately devoted to the literary qualities of their subjects' minds. They are of the psychological, not of the æsthetic order of criticism.

'There are,' to quote myself elsewhere, 'two ' methods of studying literary productions, which

' may be roughly described as the æsthetic and
' the psychological. The former goes straight to
' the literary products themselves, and seeks to
' determine their aptitude for exerting the specific
' literary emotions often reflecting the critic's own
' feelings in the rhythm and beauty of his language.
' This is the method of Lamb and Mr. Swinburne,
' and (in his best moments) Mr. Matthew Arnold.
' The other or psychological method looks rather
' to the literary producer, and endeavours to ascer-
' tain those qualities of the author's mind that
' would produce such and such results. Mr. Leslie
' Stephen pursued this method during his *Hours*
' *in a Library,* and Mr. Morley and Mr. Hutton
' afford other instances of its use.' I need scarcely
say to which of these two methods the present
essays belong. By natural bent, by training—I
have some claims to be an expert in psychology—I
belong to the psychological school. To be of the
æsthetic school is only given to those who are
something more than critics. They are the artists
in criticism; *nous autres* must be content with
being scientific, though even we may attempt to
give such artistic form to our work as science
allows. Each school has its province. I have
tried to show above that the psychological method
has a fit application at moments when we are
thinking of the literary qualities of an author's
mind rather than the literary effect of his works.

In making my estimates of George Eliot, Matthew Arnold, Browning, and Newman, I have had the critical advantage, though the personal loss, of not being personally acquainted with the subjects of my essays except in one case. Of George Eliot I may say at least *vidi tantum*. I can still recall the feelings of ardent reverence with which I approached the Priory, North Bank, one Sunday afternoon in 1877. I had written an enthusiastic—I fear I must add gushing—defence of *Daniel Deronda*, from a Jewish point of view, in the June number of *Macmillan's Magazine* of that year, and George Henry Lewes had expressed a wish that I should call upon them. I went with all the feelings of the neophyte at the shrine for the first time. Need I say that I was disappointed? Authors give of their best in their works under the consciousness of addressing the whole world. We ought not to expect them to live up to that best at all times and before all onlookers : but we do.

I have few Boswellisms to offer. I remember being struck even at that early stage of my social discernment by the contrast between the boisterous Bohemian *bonhomie* of George Lewes and the almost old-maidenish refinement of his life's companion. I had tried to lead her talk to my own criticism, but was met by the quiet parry, 'I never read criticisms of my own works.' I could not help thinking at the time ' *que fais-je donc dans cette galère ?* ' but she was obviously in the right. Others were present and the topics had to be general. We got upon songs for singing, and I was attempting to contend that the sweetest songs for vocal purposes were nowadays not those of the poets of the day. She pointed out that even Tennyson's in the *Princess* were unsuitable for that purpose, whereas the Elizabethans produced songs that were gems of literary art, yet trilled forth as naturally as a bird's carol.

I saw her but once more after Lewes's death. I had sent **her** something I had published in the *Nineteenth Century,* and she had written asking me **to call. I did so,** and found the house in gloom and herself in depression. On this occasion I was struck by the massiveness of the head as contrasted with the frailty of the body. When she was seated one thought her tall : such a head should have been propped up by a larger frame. The long thin sensitive hands were those of a musician. The exquisite modulations of the voice told of refinement in every well-chosen phrase. She had **at** least one of the qualifications one expects in an author ; she did indeed 'talk like a book.' She spoke of one **of** her favourite themes, the appeal of the circle in which one is born even if one has in certain ways grown beyond or outside it. Before I left she asked me to find out for her the meaning of a Hebrew inscription on a seal which an old Russian Jew had given Tourgenief : he had sent her an impression, which she intrusted to me. ' You will be careful of it,' she said, ' I prize it as coming from him.' I thought of old Kalonymos and his similar caution as he hands the key of his family archives to Daniel Deronda. We parted, and I soon returned the impression with an explanation of the inscription. She sent a few words of kindly thanks, and that was all till I received the final summons to Highgate Cemetery.

I do not think that my critical estimate of George Eliot's work was at all affected by this slight personal intercourse with her. My veneration for her work in those days may have led me to some extent, however, to that curious kind of injustice, when we guard against too high praise of those we know or like just because we know and like them. My personal estimate of her work when I wrote about it was certainly higher than my written words would imply. Judged by the result I was justified in this critical caution. In the ten years or so that have elapsed since her death, George Eliot's reputation has not risen, her influence has been on the decline. It seems worth while seeking for the causes of this.

It is of course a general law that literary reputations do decline for a time at least after an author's death. While he lives there is always the

halo and attraction of the unknown about what may still come from him : this fades away with his death. Then again his friends have no longer the same motives for keeping his reputation at the highest **pitch.** Friends, too, **die** away. London again is the fount of literary reputation, and Londoners, like all inhabitants of great cities, are always eager for some new thing. Old writers compete with the new ones, it is true, but the competition of the novelty is still more efficacious.

All these causes have co-operated to lessen George Eliot's influence and reputation. But there are other more special causes that have tended in the same direction. Mr. Cross's *Life* was **a** disappointment: his extreme reticence about personal details and careful excision of all humanising touches made the book dull, and the total impression of George Eliot's personality unattractive. Her last books, *Daniel Deronda, Theophrastus Such,* and the collected *Essays,* were a progressive series of anti-climaxes, and it is the latest works that give the final impression in more senses than one. Their didactic tone was too obvious, and the British public resents nothing more than being preached at too obviously.

But above and beyond all these reasons there has been a subtle and gradual change in the public mind which **has** told against George Eliot's work in two directions. There is a fashion in the art of

the novel, as in other arts, **and for some time**
the vogue has been growing for the *conte* as
against the novel, and **for** the romantic novel of
incident as against the realistic novel of character.
Amid the problems and perplexities of the present
we fly for relaxation to the Something-other-than-
Here-and-Now, and we like to take it short. Both
tendencies tell against George Eliot. There **is**
a general tendency nowadays against taking intellectual nourishment in anything but small doses.
The enormous growth of the magazines is at once
a result and a cause of this. *Tit-Bits* completes
what **the** *Fortnightly Review* began. It is indeed
an Age of Tit-bits. The strenuous attention which
the works of George Eliot demand is too much for
minds accustomed to such intellectual food as the
magazines now supply. The high seriousness of
her art displeases the frivolous, and the tone of
English Letters just now is distinctly frivolous.

George Eliot aimed and claimed to be a teacher.
Her works were a conscious criticism of life.
They gave the new feeling about life that seemed to
be rendered necessary by the triumph of Darwinism in English speculation. During the 'seventies'
there was a confident feeling, among those of us
who came to our intellectual majority in those
years, that Darwinism was to solve all the problems. This was doubtless due to the triumphant tone in which certain eminent professors of

science—notably Professors Huxley, Tyndall, and Clifford—spoke of what science was going to do for the spiritual life when the older theological trammels had been removed. What they promised George Eliot was currently supposed to have attained, and her words were scanned for the secret message. She was to all of us what she seemed to Mr. F. W. Myers in that fine description of his interview with her in the Fellows' Garden at Trinity; she was 'a Sibyl in the gloom.' She alone, we thought, possessed the message of the New Spirit that Darwinism was to breathe into the inner life of man.

Well, Darwinism has come, and has conquered, and, as a vital influence in the spiritual life, has gone. Instead of solving all the problems, it has raised only too many fresh ones. It has thrown light on origins, or to speak more accurately, it has set us on the search for origins. But the undeveloped germ which we call origin has in it *ex hypothesi* all the problems which the developed product offers, and presents these in more concentrated form. And the something that develops is obviously different from its own development, which is all that Darwinism even professes to explain. To put it technically, origins are not essences, and it is the essence of the matter, the thing as in itself it really is, that we seek for. Hence Darwinism, which merely touches origins and leaves essences alone, only disappoints. The pretty quarrel, too, that is going on among the experts about the fundamentals of Darwinism has helped to discredit it. And with this discredit George Eliot, **the** literary voice of Darwinism, suffers **too**. The danger which I foresaw in 1879—'the risk of subordinating the eternal truths of art to what may be the temporary opinions of science '—**has** proved to be no illusory one.

Again our interests have turned from speculation, even from **the** bases of conduct, and are **almost** exclusively social. 'We are all socialists now'— since the Redistribution Act—and George Eliot has little to say on the Condition of England Question. **And** what little she does say, in *Felix Holt* for example, is not much in consonance with the feeling of to-day. Her dearest memories were of a **time when** old Leisure was still alive and social changes **took** place but slowly. Felix Holt the Radical **is** rather Felix Holt the Conservative ; he **is** not even a Tory-Democrat. But the ineffectiveness of her social utterances was a sign that her heart was not in the social part of her work ; we have no heart for anything else.

For all these reasons then the reputation **of** George Eliot is undergoing a kind of eclipse in this **last** decade of the nineteenth century. It is becoming **safe** to indulge in cheap sneers at the ineffectiveness of her heroes, at the want of *élan* in

the movement of her **stories,** at the too obvious
preachments **of** her rather overspun comments.
Her heroes are perhaps rather apt to be muffs ; it
is the way with heroes of novels generally. Her
plots might develop at greater speed ; your novel
of character rarely travels express. 'Here the
story halts a little' might be written over many a
page of Richardson and Fielding, of Miss Austen
and Thackeray, but it is a part of their method and
a necessary part. And the comments and discussion
which cause these frequent halts, have they not
a special appeal **of** their own, even if the appeal
be somewhat alien to the art of the novel? And
if George Eliot preaches, what admirable sermons
she writes ! The realistic writer cannot describe
the life around him or her without indicating the
attitude they take towards it. That very attitude
is a preachment: Zola in *L'Assommoir,* Flaubert
in *Madame Bovary,* are as powerful sermons **as I**
know.

That part then of George Eliot's work which ap-
pealed more especially to the *Zeitgeist* is ineffective
now that the *Zeitgeist* **has** changed. But how
much remains that can never lose its effectiveness
because it appeals to the *ewige Geist* **of** humanity.
Her admirable peasants and parsons, her charming
children, her scenery and her interiors, **her** wit
and her wisdom, these are surely a possession for
aye **in** the realm of English **fiction.** Whatever

view we take of her art, we must recognise that she
has added as many living personalities to the common acquaintance of English-speaking people as
almost any other English novelist, and this after
all is the final criterion.   And in the difficult
sphere of the aphorism, her works are more
copiously studded with subtle truths aptly expressed than those of any novelist who has ever
written in English.   The enemy will say this has
nothing to do with the novel : but the enemy can
always complain of any form of art that it is not
another, so we may let him sneer.

It has seemed worth while devoting some attention to the after-history of George Eliot's reputation, as so much of this volume happens already to
be taken up by a consideration of George Eliot's
art from various points of view, and I have here
attempted to complete the survey.   With the other
authors considered, there is no occasion to deal
in such detail, as their loss is so recent that any
attempt to distinguish the permanent elements of
their art would be impracticable.

I may add that I have found a difficulty in giving
an appropriate name to these studies, so far as they
are not reviews.   'Obituaries' of the authors they
are not, for I do not profess to give any details of
their lives, or even of their works.   'Necrologe'
does not sound English, and besides savours of
Woking.   *Éloge* comes nearest, but that on the

face of it is not English. A wicked wag among my friends suggests *Post Mortems*, but I trust I have not been quite so cruel as that would imply.

One more word and I have done. There seems something of ingratitude, almost of irreverence, in subjecting to cool criticism writers to whom one owes so much of one's best self. I need not refute the fallacy, that in presuming to criticise one assumes any superiority : if that were so, there would scarcely be any place for criticism, and certainly none at all for critics *pur sang*. The author appeals to his generation: the critic answers the appeal. In the present case the thing had to be done and I was called upon to do it. I can only say I tried to do my work as honestly and conscientiously as was in my power.

GEORGE ELIOT

December 22, 1880

A

GEORGE ELIOT

EVENTEEN years ago the Christmas week was darkened by the death of Thackeray. Once again the festive season has been saddened in many a household by the knowledge that George Eliot was no more. It is not too much to say that with many her works have been far more than novels; they have formed an animating principle co-operating with some of the most powerful spiritual influences of the time. It appears, therefore, to be an appropriate occasion to pass in critical review the works she has left behind her and to estimate their importance.

As is well known, her earlier productions were translations of German works on the metaphysics of religion. Strauss's *Life of Jesus* appeared in an English form in 1846, and Feuerbach's *Essence of Christianity* in 1853. As translations they were excellent, but it cannot be said that they have had any

influence on English speculation. Their chief
interest consists in the evidence they give of
George Eliot's early devotion to 'advanced'
thinking and absorbing interest in the philosophy of religion.

Her importance in the history of English
literature rests upon the series of fictions
commenced in 1857 with the *Scenes of Clerical
Life*, and concluded in 1876 by *Daniel
Deronda*. It is not difficult to discern in
these works two widely varying sets of artistic
motives. The *Scenes*, *Adam Bede* (1859),
The Mill on the Floss, *Silas Marner*, *Felix Holt*,
and *Middlemarch* are all clearly connected by
their subject-matter, and, in large measure, by
their style of treatment. In them she went
back to the scenes and days of her childhood. It has been often remarked that the
plastic period of the literary artist, when
impressions are retained with that minute
observation necessary for the novel, ceases at
an extremely early age. Dickens was only at
home in the England of coaches and among
the lower classes. George Eliot was most
happy when recalling mid-England in the
days before the Reform Bill. Her father was
a land surveyor, and she thus came in contact
with all classes of provincial society, so that
her pictures are far more complete than either
Dickens's or Thackeray's accounts of London

life. **Both** George Eliot and George **Sand**
had learned that provincial **life is more**
intense, if more monotonous and simple, than
the busy life of towns. Amid the turmoil **of**
cities, existence passes through **a** series **of**
shallows, **as** it were ; whereas in the country
the emotions are collected **into** one deep
pool, which pours forth tumultuously if **once**
disturbed. Throughout these novels of
memory, as they may **be** termed, the incidents and **tone** have **a** tragic ring **about**
them which is wanting in the majority **of**
novels dealing with London life. Only **in**
the Brontës, and perhaps in Mrs. Gaskell, **do**
we find anything like the depth of earnestness displayed in these novels of George
Eliot. Much of their piquancy depends on
the contrast between the subject-matter and
the manifold reflections to which it gives rise.
While the subject is entirely obsolete, the reflections are in accord with the most advanced
thought of the day. Every one knows something of the scenery and the characters amid
which these novels are placed. The **rich**
fields of Loamshire **and** their owners and
cultivators in the early years of this cen-
tury form the common background of these
tragedies of human life. Generally speaking,
they treat of the influence of adverse circumstance on **the** inner life **of the actors.**

It is essentially the spiritual life of her heroes
and heroines which interests the writer. It
is characteristic that she has introduced the
religious life as a leading motive of the novel.
Dinah Morris's spiritual experiences and ex-
hortations, Maggie Tulliver's conversion by
Thomas à Kempis, even Mr. Bulstrode's
wrestlings of the spirit, are themes which
only the deepest spiritual sympathy could
have handled adequately. Not that she is
deficient in the lighter qualities of the
novelist's art. No one has described English
scenery with more accurate touch or displayed
a more Shakespearean sense of humour. Mrs.
Poyser and Bartle Massey are unequalled
creations. In the delineation of children's
character she stands almost on a level with
Victor Hugo. Altogether, in range of sympathy, in nobility of tone, in fertility of
reflection, and in subtlety of insight these
novels of memory are unique in the history
of fiction. Opinion will differ as to their
comparative merits, and each has its distinctive qualities. Yet it is probable that *Adam
Bede* will always retain a certain supremacy ;
there is a freshness of tone as if the writer
were luxuriating in new-found powers. The
unsavoury *motif* of *Felix Holt* places it out of
competition ; *Silas Marner,* finished as it is, is
on a smaller scale ; and the concluding part

of *The Mill* on *the Floss* destroys the **almost**
perfect ' artistry ' **of the story of** Tom **and**
Maggie Tulliver. *Middlemarch* remains, and
as ' a study in provincial life ' is complete ; yet
the deficiencies in the plot and a certain
undercurrent of social protest counterbalance
its other advantages, and the palm is left to
George Eliot's first **and probably greatest**
work. The **subject of** *Adam Bede* **required**
extreme **delicacy of** treatment ; **but all** such
requirements **are** satisfied. **The** shallowness
of Hetty's character removes from her that
sympathy which would otherwise render her
fate too sad for the imagination ; but her
history illustrates the lesson which all these
novels were consciously made to teach. They
aided the great work of Wordsworth in
educating the emotions to sympathise with
the fundamental joys and sorrows of human
life in all social spheres. **And in** the fine
words of Wordsworth about **his own** works,
' **They** will co-operate with the benign **ten-**
' dencies in nature and society, and will, in
' their degree, be efficacious in **making men**
' wiser, better, and happier.'

The remaining novels, *Romola*, **The** *Spanish
Gypsy* (apart from its unfortunate form), and
Daniel *Deronda*, deal with an entirely different
range of interests. They are romances of the
historic imagination, consciously creative **in-**

stead of being, as in the other novels, unconsciously reproductive. The first two dealt
with the history of the past, and one cannot
help thinking that *The Spanish Gypsy* would
have been almost as successful a reproduction
as *Romola* if it had been written in a congenial
medium. In these laborious research did the
work that loving memory effected in the other
novels. As the artist went to work more
consciously, so the motive principle of her
work came more to the surface. The leading
conception of modern science as applied to
man, the influence of hereditary transmission,
was transmuted into the moral principle of
the claims of race. In the novels of memory
this had been disguised under the simpler
form of family love. Maggie Tulliver's action
at the end of *The Mill on the Floss* is entirely
based on the claims of family as opposed to
personal affection for Stephen Guest. ' Love
is *not* enough' is the refrain, and this comes
out still more strongly on the broader historic
canvas of *Romola* and *The Spanish Gypsy*.
The point of Tito Melema's treachery is the
absence of hereditary connection with Floren-
tine politics. Fedalma sacrifices everything
to the claims of race. In *Daniel Deronda* the
difficult task was attempted of raising contemporary events to a *quasi*-historic level. By
the mere force of genius George Eliot strove

to create a personality which she deliberately asserted to be on a level with the great spiritual leaders of mankind. We have reasons for saying that the identification of the Jewish prophet of *Daniel Deronda* with a philosophic Jew described by Mr. G. H. Lewes in the *Fortnightly Review* is erroneous. The Jews give the greatest example in modern times of fidelity to the claims of race, and it was natural that George Eliot should have sympathised with Jewish aspirations. In *The Spanish Gypsy* she had already portrayed a fine figure in the Jew Sephardo. In Mordecai Cohen she attempted to idealise the history of this remarkable race, and by so doing destroyed the chances of success for her most elaborate production. Want of knowledge and want of sympathy with the Jewish ideal will probably always be an effectual bar to the appreciation of *Daniel Deronda*, and the hero plays the difficult part of irradiating sympathy instead of doing noble deeds. Yet it would be rash to assert that, if the Jewish race again became prominent as a nationality, *Daniel Deronda* may not ultimately figure as one of the favourite books of the Chosen People. Even as it is, it must be recognised that the conception of such a character as the principal Jew of the book shows singular artistic daring.

While *Romola* and *Daniel Deronda* are of a different *genre* from the other novels, they have a share of their excellences of style and characterisation. Since attention was first drawn to the point, too much stress has been laid on the 'scientific technicalities' of her style of late years. She would not have been the foremost woman of her age if she had not been influenced by one of its greatest movements. Yet the evidences of this are as clear in her earliest as in her latest works. In *Janet's Repentance* we read that 'the idea of 'duty . . . is to the moral life what the 'addition of a great central ganglion is to 'animal life.' In the second page of *Adam Bede*, Seth's 'coronal arch' becomes a prominent feature in his portrait. In *The Mill on the Floss* George Eliot cannot let us know the ingenious trick by which Bob Jakin gains a couple of inches in measuring out his flannel without referring to his thumb as the 'mark of difference between the man and the monkey.' It is not quite correct to say that her style became more scientific in her last two novels; it would be more exact to say that it became more complex. As her thoughts became more subtle, her sentences naturally became more complex, and it would be difficult to determine the limits beyond which subtlety and complexity become inartistic. Allied to this error is the statement, frequently repeated in the obituary notices of the **newspapers,** that George Eliot was essentially an analytic genius, and that she constructed her characters **out** of analytic materials. The idea immediately suggested by this curiously uncritical assertion is that the perusal **of** Mr. Bain's works is the best propædeutic for the **creation** of a character like **Dolly** Winthrop. It would be far more correct to say **that** George Eliot's genius was essentially constructive, and that **her** analytic comments are the results of her training **and** experience. Like all great moderns, George Eliot possessed the power of feeling deeply and of simultaneously **intel-** lectualising her feelings; this is the most characteristic note of the modern mind. **In** this regard **it** is interesting to notice her accuracy and completeness, which at first sight appear peculiarly scientific. **Yet** it is the selective accuracy **of the** artist, not the exhaustive exactness of the *savant,* that **she** displays. When Cabel **Garth's** eyebrows ' make their pathetic angle ' we have this trait alone given, and not a paragraph from Mr. Darwin's *Expression of the Emotions.* It would perhaps be more appropriate to point **to** her stern adherence to the fact of human nature as answering to the accuracy and impartiality **of** the scientific **mind.** Maggie

Tulliver's sudden love for a dandy like Stephen Guest may grate against Mr. Swinburne's **critical** feelings, but is, no doubt, true to human nature. It is this fidelity to the facts of life that gives the prominent sadness to her works. She has chosen tragic themes, **and** tragic events are apt to be sad. Perhaps the most dominant idea of her *Weltanschauung* is the conception **of** law in human character.

> Our deeds still travel with us from afar,
> And what we have been makes us what we are,

might stand as a motto to all her works.

It is character **in process** of change that engages all **her interest.** Hence there is less **of** the conventional, less of **the** worldly, in **her work** than in most great novelists. We have soul speaking to soul: Dinah to Hetty, Savonarola to Romola, Felix to Esther, Dorothea to Ladislaw, Mordecai to Deronda. When the conventional is introduced it is chiefly for humorous purposes; the humour of the immortal scene at the Rainbow Inn in *Silas Marner* consists in its archaic conventionality. Interest of character is, however, the predominant interest of George Eliot's work. Nearly one-half of *Adam Bede* is taken up **by** the first **week of the** action, during which **we learn to** know the chief characters. The rest of the book hurries through nearly two years before Adam is united to Dinah. This attention to characterisation has exercised a somewhat deleterious effect on her plots; so long as we know what her characters are and have become, it does not so much matter what becomes of them. Hence the frequent resource to the *Deus ex machinâ* of sudden death; it is astonishing how many of her characters are snatched from our view in this way. Death by drowning seems to be the favourite method: Dunstan Cass, Tom and Maggie Tulliver, Tito Melema, Grandcourt, all disappear in this abrupt way. It would be unjust to pass from this aspect of her work without a word of praise to her admirable range of power, and to the marvellous ability she possessed of giving life to her minor characters. The moral earnestness of her work is another prominent 'note.' With her the novel was morality teaching by example. And the teaching was of an unusually lofty character. Renunciation of self, subordination to the social life, were the great texts. Egoism is the canker of the soul: Hetty, Tito Melema, Grandcourt, are prominent examples. Still more noteworthy is the terrible example of the crippling of another's life by one's egoism, as in Rosamund Vincy and Lydgate, to whom Casaubon and Dorothea form so fine a parallel and contrast. The moral of *The Spanish Gypsy* lies in the ruin wrought to the great schemes of Zarca by the egoistic loves of Silva and Fedalma. The whole aim of the novel as George Eliot wrote it might be summed up in the words, κάθαρσις of egoism.

The whole artistic career was dominated by these ethical aims; in her last work, *The Impressions of Theophrastus Such*, she applied herself consciously to direct ethical teaching. The book consists of disconnected examples of popular moral errors from which George Eliot would free the world, 'debasing the moral currency,' 'the modern Hep! Hep! Hep!' and so on. As a consequence, the artistic merits of *Theophrastus Such* were far below those of her other books, and it will never have much more than a pathological interest for the student of her works.

It remains to speak of her attempts in verse. George Eliot will always afford a striking example of the truth that the essential quality of the poet is the gift of song. All the other qualities required for poetry were possessed by her in high measure, yet it is granted on all sides that her poetical attempts were failures. The 'brother and sister' sonnets and the Comtean hymn, 'O may I join the choir invisible!' in the *Jubal* volume, a speech of Zarca's ('Nay, never falter'), and a fine description of Truth by Sephardo in *The Spanish Gypsy*, with, perhaps, Ladislaw's song, 'Oh me, oh me, what frugal cheer my love doth feed upon!'—these may find a place in anthologies, but that is all.

Writing now with the sense of her loss still fresh, it is impossible to forget that, for those who knew her personally, she herself was her greatest work. By her own training she made herself probably the most accomplished woman the century has seen. She brought to the world of art a greater extent of culture than any predecessor, with the possible exception of Goethe. Not alone was she a veritable pundit in languages, with mastery of French, German, and Italian, and serviceable knowledge of Latin, Greek, Spanish, and Hebrew; she was widely learned in science and philosophy, and deeply read in history; her works teem with evidence of her intimate knowledge of music and painting. Add to all these accomplishments a width of sympathy and acuteness of observation seldom equalled, and one can form some idea of the rich nature just taken from us. She could draw such characters as Maggie Tulliver and Dorothea Brooke, Mary Garth and Gwendolen Harleth, Fedalma and Romola, because she

herself had much that was present in them. She has done a great deal for the cause of woman by direct teaching, **but** she has done most by giving the world assurance of the possibilities of woman's excellence.

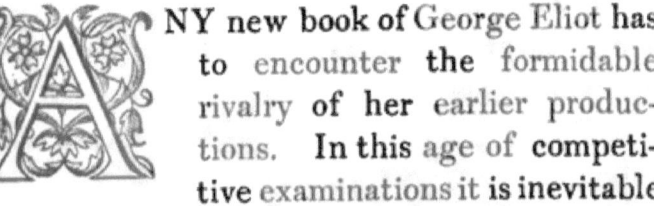NY new book of George Eliot has to encounter the formidable rivalry of her earlier productions. In this age of competitive examinations it is inevitable that some attempt should be made to 'place' the new work in its 'order of merit.' Such a test, however, tells with crushing force against the *Impressions of Theophrastus Such*, which is slighter in conception, less finished in execution, and altogether of less artistic value than any other work that has appeared under her name. In it are seen all the characteristics of her later 'manner' which critics have had to deprecate. The scientific interest and tone of her second period culminate in these studies of mental pathology. The consummate literary artist has degenerated into the student of social psychology.

George Eliot's literary development falls clearly and sharply into two stages. In the earlier period, from the *Scenes of Clerical Life* to *Felix Holt* (with the exception of *Romola*, which stands apart in a sphere of its own, where *The Spanish Gypsy*, had it been written in a natural medium, might have joined it), she went back with loving memory to the days and scenes of her childhood. In that wonderful series of works she produced living pictures of mid-England in the pre-Reform days before old Leisure was dead, and while the modern spirit was unborn. For width of conception, for accuracy of touch, for nobility of tone, those works have a place apart in English fiction. The next two novels, *Middlemarch* and *Daniel Deronda*, displayed a new set of literary motives in their composition. The loving interest of the artist in human nature was fused with the intellectual interest of the scientific observer of the social organism. The tales moved in a larger sphere, had a wider scope, and also a deeper background than the earlier works. A new view of the relations of man and society, and with it a new philosophy of history, informed every page and set every incident in a new light. Along with this change or development of tone there went a noticeable change of manner. Dealing with conceptions novel to her readers, George Eliot had to put them directly before their eyes in passages only interesting from a speculative point of view. But this very need of explanation argued incomplete 'artistry' (to use a word of Mr.

Browning's); **there** was evidently **not that** direct *rapport* with her audience which **is a necessary** pre-requisite **of all great literary art.** However well **suited Comtean concep-tions may** be for appeals **to** the literary **emotions,** such appeals **cannot** fail to be less telling when accompanied **by elaborate ex-**planations of the conceptions **upon** which their efficacy depends. This reflective or scientific side of her later **works has** seriously diminished their effectiveness, and the attempt to rouse an interest in the history of modern Judaism in *Daniel Deronda* was, with the ordinary reader, a complete failure. And it must be remembered that in really great works of art the decision rests with the 'ordinary reader'; success is here the real **test of** merit. No poem is great if only a small coterie admire it. What is **to** be the decision on George Eliot's last two great works depends upon the future of the specula-tive system **with which** they are connected. If the social philosophy there taught be that **of** the future, then *Middlemarch* and *Daniel Deronda* may become **as** gospels. But the risk has been run of subordinating the eternal truths of art to what may be the temporary **opinions** of science; and, in any case, the presence of the purely analytical element in her later works must necessarily detract from their **artistic** value **as indicating** a certain spiritual divergence of George Eliot from her readers. As a matter of fact, the intellectual or scientific element in the last two works did alienate her audience's sympathy, and thus frustrated the artist's function, to ' arrest, arouse, and excite.'

This scientific element comes **to a** head in *Theophrastus Such*. Instead of **a new novel,** George Eliot has given us some careful but unsympathetic analyses of certain phases **of human** character : admirable dissections, no doubt; **but** life has fled under the scalpel. Our emotions **refuse to** be moved by a description **of** Aliquis or Quispiam ; and, what is more, the **author** herself fails **to** feel the artist's sympathy with her creations. The pathos of Merman's struggle against the errors of Grampus, in the section entitled ' How we encourage Research,' is nullified by a certain kindly contempt which finds expression in some rather Teutonic **or** ' cetacean ' witticisms. And throughout there **is a** tendency to harshness in censure which is not to be found in the writer's more extended works. The whole book **is devoted** to the **foibles and** failings **of** man, and thus leaves an unpleasant feeling. The head, not the heart, has produced this book, **the** reader feels, and **his** heart fails to respond to pure intellect. **It** is worthy of note that most of the sketches

deal with phases of literary life which have
been the object of George Eliot's mature and
conscious observation. It would seem that
the novelist's plastic period closes at an early
age : Dickens was never at home with railways,
George Eliot as an artist feels strange after
the Reform Bill is passed. Of later London
life she has, no doubt, been an observant
spectator, but there is the greatest possible
difference shown in the reproductions in her
earliest and latest work : spontaneous art in
the *Scenes of Clerical Life*, conscious effort in
these Sketches of Literary Life. And in her
latest book the nearest approach to the manner
of her first period is displayed in the supposed
autobiographical recollections of Mr. Such
when he is ' looking back ' to ' the time when
' the fitful gleams of a spring day used to show
' me my own shadow as that of a small boy on
' a small pony, riding by the side of a larger
' cob-mounted shadow over the breezy up-
' lands which we used to dignify with the
' name of hills, or along by-roads with broad
' grassy borders and hedgerows reckless of
' utility, on our way to outlying hamlets,
' whose groups of inhabitants were as distinct
' to my imagination as if they had belonged
' to different regions of the globe.'

The passages descriptive of earlier England
in the same section are in her very best style,

and contrast markedly with the first section,
'Looking Inward,' where the pseudonymous
writer analyses with subtle skill his claims as
a scientific observer and describer of other
men's failings. The following quotation shows
the old manner :—

   'Our rural tracts—where **no** Babel-
'chimney scales **the** heavens—are without
' mighty objects to fill the soul with the sense
' of an outer world unconquerably aloof from
' our efforts.   The wastes **are** playgrounds
' (and let **us try to keep** them such for the
' children's children who will inherit no other
' sort of demesne); the grasses and reeds nod
' **to each other** over **the** river, but we have
' cut a canal **close by ;** the very heights laugh
' with corn **in** August or lift the plough-team
' **against** the sky in September.   Then comes
' a crowd of burly navvies with pickaxes and
' barrows, and while hardly a wrinkle is made
' in the fading mother's face or a new curve
' of health in the blooming girl's, the hills are
' **cut** through or the breaches between them
' spanned, we choose our level, and **the white**
' steam-pennon flies **along it.   But** because
' our land shows this readiness to be changed,
' **all signs of permanence** upon it raise a tender
' **attachment** instead **of awe :** some of us, at
' least, love **the scanty relics** of our forests,
' and are thankful if **a** bush is left of the old

' hedgerow. A crumbling bit of wall where
' the delicate ivy-leafed toad-flax hangs its
' light branches, or a bit of grey thatch with
' patches of dark moss on its shoulder and
' a troop of grass-stems on its ridge, is a
' thing to visit. And then the tiled roof of
' cottage and homestead, of the long cow-shed
' where generations of the milky mothers
' have stood patiently, of the broad-shouldered
' barns where the old-fashioned flail once made
' resonant music, while the watch-dog barked
' at the timidly venturesome fowls making
' pecking raids on the outflying grain—the
' roofs that have looked out from among the
' elms and walnut-trees, or beside the yearly
' group of hay and corn stacks, or below the
' square stone steeple, gathering their grey
' or ochre-tinted lichens and their olive-green
' mosses under all ministries,—let us praise
' the sober harmonies they give to our land-
' scape, helping to unite us pleasantly with
' the elder generations who tilled the soil for
' us before we were born, and paid heavier
' and heavier taxes, with much grumbling,
' but without that deepest root of corruption
' —the self-indulgent despair which cuts down
' and consumes and never plants.'

The next quotation illustrates the new
style :—

' Introspection which starts with the pur-

' **pose of finding** out one's own absurdities is not
' **likely** to be very mischievous, yet of course
' it is not **free** from dangers any more than
' **breathing is, or** the other functions that keep
' us alive and active. To judge **of** others by
' one's-self is in its most innocent meaning
' the briefest expression for **our** only method
' **of** knowing mankind ; yet we perceive it has
' come to mean in many cases either the
' vulgar mistake which reduces every man's
' value to the very low figure at which **the**
' valuer himself happens to stand ; **or** else, the
' amiable illusion of the higher nature misled
' **by a** too generous construction of the lower.
' One cannot give a recipe for wise judgment :
' **it** resembles appropriate muscular action,
' which **is** attained by the myriad lessons in
' nicety of balance and of aim that only
' practice can give. The danger of the in-
' verse procedure, judging of self by what one
' observes in others, if it is carried on with
' much impartiality and keenness of discern-
' ment, **is** that it has a laming effect, enfeeb-
' ling the energies of indignation and scorn,
' which are the proper scourges of wrong-doing
' and meanness, and which should continually
' feed the wholesome restraining power of
' public opinion.'

In terming these *Impressions* scientific, we
do not **mean** to say that they **are** written

in any scientific jargon ; indeed, we have less
of sesquipedalian technicalities than in *Daniel
Deronda* ; but the whole tone is scientific.
Without indulging in any such elaborate
antitheses as are the glory of the schoolboy's
essay, it may be said that the artistic and
scientific modes of treating human nature
differ in this, that science seeks to find general
analogies, while art aims at individual realities. The sketchy character of these studies
no doubt brings into greater prominence their
want of artistic reality. If the author had
elaborated any of them into novels or even
into ' scenes,' the artist instinct would have
given life to the dead bones of scientific
analysis. And what is more, the reader would
have been spared that unsympathy with her
own puppets which may be scientific impartiality, but is certainly inartistic harshness.
Humour would then have dealt tenderly with
those deficiencies which wit, and that of a
somewhat lumbering character, now mercilessly
exposes. One of the sections deals with the
habit of scoffing and parody as ' debasing the
moral currency,' yet what is it but debasing
the artistic currency to ring the changes on
Grampus, Lord Narwhal, Prof. Sperm N.
Whale, Dugong, and Butzkopf (= *Delphinus
orca*)? The name Merman brings into humorous contrast his more human qualities ; but is

not the 'ancient and fish-like smell' with which Teutonic erudition is, by implication, connected in these appellatives, just a case of 'debasing the moral currency' in its depreciation of the minute accuracy and unselfish devotion of German scholarship? Indeed, the names throughout throw much light on the characters of the book. In most cases they represent exactly that particular phase of a character which is brought forward, the limb which is to represent the whole figure. We can all guess beforehand to what sort of characters names like Touchwood, Mordax, and Scintilla will be applied. The more individual the name the more of the uncertainty of real life about the character: that will be found to be a good working test. Thus Pummel, who serves in some inexplicable way as a 'watchdog of knowledge,' stands out well defined. 'What is the cause of the tides, 'Pummel?' 'Well, sir, nobody rightly knows. 'Many gives their opinion, but if I was to 'give mine, it 'ud be different.' That is a touch worthy of the hand that drew Mrs. Poyser and Dolly Winthrop.

And as the scientific spirit shows itself in these unreal abstractions of truncated characters, so we have it again in the manner of their presentation. The inordinate length of the sentences and the frequent obscurity of sense are other symptoms **of the same** characteristic. Science abhors **the epigram ; its** half-truth, though it may be the better half **of** truth, is repugnant to the exactness of science. For purposes of science we must have **all** the amplifications and exceptions necessary **for** accuracy, and consequently we must have long and unwieldy sentences. In *Theophrastus Such* we have noticed **one sentence** dragging its laborious length over twenty-two lines, and we **reckon the** average length at about eight lines. In one place **it** takes two whole pages (pp. 288, 289) to complete four sentences. Another ' note ' of the scientific style is its tendency **to** draw out all the attenuated meaning of **a** sentence. We have many instances of sentences which contain truths that are tolerably obvious, in phraseology by no means obvious **to a first reading.** The book **throughout is** hard **reading, and the** style **at times** harsh in the extreme ; **what a falling off from the** limpid truths **of her earlier books !** **Even in** *Daniel Deronda* the reader comes across **such** fine things as ' Those who trust us educate us ' —a noble truth, nobly expressed. He **will** have difficulty **in** finding a single sentence in **this book** which is worthy to be put by its side.

The artistic value of **the book is further** spoiled **by its** evident didactic **purpose. If** the characters here delineated **do not** ' adorn

a tale,' they are certainly intended to 'point
a moral.' Throughout George Eliot's literary
career ethical interests have been predominant.
With her the novel has been morality teaching
by example. But hitherto she has been content
with the subtle insinuation of the artist, and
has left alone the direct assault of the preacher;
she has given texts, not sermons. But in her
last book there is rather too much direct
preaching; it might be a little hard, but it
would not be altogether untrue, to call the
Impressions skeleton sermons. Even from
the ethical point of view the result is unsatis-
factory; how much less effective a lesson is
taught by Mixtus than by Lydgate in *Middlemarch*, though this is partly due to necessarily lighter treatment. With the character
of her teaching every one is now familiar.
Subordinate yourself to the social organism,
suppress self; this is her ever-recurring cry.
All honour to the nobleness and purity of the
teaching. After all, that is the characteristic
which raises this book above all other descriptions of 'characters,' from the second book
of Aristotle's *Rhetoric* to La Bruyère; but
it comes too often to the surface, is pressed
too markedly upon our notice.

Nowhere does the inferior effectiveness of
the intellectual as compared with the artistic
treatment of a subject come into greater

prominence than in the last chapter of the book ' The Modern Hep! Hep! Hep!' (the rallying cry of the persecutions of the Jews by the Crusaders). That George Eliot should feel tempted to defend her choice of a subject in *Daniel Deronda* is only natural; but the striking thing is how far inferior is this defence, appealing to the intellect, when compared with exactly the same arguments as urged by the passionate rhetoric of Mordecai in the book itself. Ignorance of, and want of sympathy with, modern Judaism may blind the reader to the extraordinary power of Mordecai's orations, perhaps the greatest *tour de force* of their author; but any one can see how much more effective, even from an argumentative point of view, are the passionate utterances of the latest prophet than the calm reasoning of his creator.

We have dealt with *Impressions of Theophrastus Such* in comparison with its author's other works, and it is clear that it cannot, in conception, style, or effectiveness, stand the test. It may consequently appear somewhat unfair to upbraid the book for failing to be what it does not profess to be. But a great artist owes duties to the world as much as deserves gratitude from it. When one who has it in her power to add to the world's wealth of beauty turns aside from the arduous conception of a great **work to execute** preparatory sketches **not worthy of mention** by the side of her other works, **it** is impossible to refrain from deploring the loss to the world. Let others **take** upon themselves to compare these 'characters' with similar literary **productions**; for us none but herself can be her parallel. Others may take up the half-disguised challenge of the motto from Phædrus (3 *Prol.* 45-50); we do not care to discuss whether Pepin is Mr. Gladstone or Dugong **Du Bois-**Reymond.

For us, the chief interest **in** George Eliot's **new** work has been that **which we are** confident will be its chief interest to the future students of her works. The light **thrown by** it on **the** scientific strain in her literary character, **the** light thrown upon the workmanship of her second period, give the book a sort of pathological interest to the student of literature. The choice of the autobiographical form (used only once before, in the remarkable sketch *à la* **E. A.** Poe, *The Lifted Veil*) may have **its** significance **for** the next generation. **But,** apart from these points **of view, the** studies **are** but chips from the workshop, which might **well** have been **left on** the ground, only to be lifted thence at the time when everything of **the author** shall become precious.

'ESSAYS'

 HESE essays will not add to the reputation of their author. Reprinted chiefly from the *Westminster Review*, it would be difficult to say that they stand prominently above the general average of such essays. Each of the quarterlies has created for itself a type, and these reviews are of the type familiar to us in such writers as the late W. R. Greg. They date from the period before Mr. Matthew Arnold had imported the method of Sainte-Beuve into English criticism, and in consequence they suffer by comparison with later work of a more subtle and artistic character. George Eliot's essays have not sufficient individuality to deserve new life for their own sake ; on the other hand, they throw valuable light on certain problems connected with her art, and on this account merit republication.

The collection inevitably raises what must be the chief critical problem in connection with the literary career of George Eliot. How is it, the reader is impelled to ask, that a mind which produced these essays chiefly

during the years 1855 and 1856 could have
given the *Scenes of Clerical Life* to the world
a year later? **What was the** determining
motive which changed the translator of Strauss
and Feuerbach and the writer of these essays
into the loving creator of Mr. Gilfil, of Bartle
Massey, and of Dinah Morris? It is not **so**
much the late flowering of her genius that is
noteworthy. The end of the ' thirties' seems
the appropriate period for a novelist's *début.*
Both Thackeray and Miss Austen were thirty-
seven (the same age as George Eliot in 1857)
when *Vanity Fair* and *Sense and Sensibility*
respectively appeared; Trollope was thirty-
nine when *The Warden* **was** published; and
Walter Scott was **as** old **as** forty-three when
Waverley first delighted **the** world. But all
these had given indication in one way or
another of their powers, and had certainly not
given indication of ability of quite a different
calibre and in quite an opposite tendency of
mind; whereas George Eliot up to her first
appearance as a novelist had shown marked
capacity **for** abstract thought, the very antithesis of the concrete imagination essential
for the novelist.

Up to the age **of** thirty-seven what do we
find in George Eliot's writings? A vivid
appreciation of the course of religious thought,
a considerable power **of** social generalisation,

and, above all, a deep interest in the scientific and philosophic speculations of her time. If any one had ventured a prophecy of her future **career,** he would surely have anticipated **some** incursion into the region of religious reconstruction, as was the case with her friend Miss Hennell. He might have foreseen in her another Harriet Martineau, with **a** deeper ethical basis, but with the same tendency to pure reason. The last thought **that** would have entered the minds of **her most** intimate friends up to that date would have been that Marian Evans would revive in the enduring form of art the reminiscences of her early days, which she seemed to have left so **far** behind her.

Certainly the essays before us indicated no such **future.** One of them, indeed, dealing with **the** *Natural History of German Life,* proves **that** George Eliot had observed as closely **the** English peasant **as** her author Riehl had studied the German species. Take the following picture :—

'Observe a company **of** haymakers. **When** 'you see them at a distance, tossing up the 'forkfuls of hay in the golden light, while the 'waggon creeps slowly with its increasing 'burthen over the meadow, and the bright 'green **space** which tells of work done gets 'larger **and** larger, you pronounce the scene

c

' "smiling," and you think these companions
' in labour must be as bright and cheerful as
' the picture to which they give animation.
' Approach nearer, and you will certainly find
' that haymaking time is a time for joking,
' especially if there are women among the
' labourers; but the coarse laugh that bursts
' out every now and then, and expresses the
' triumphant taunt, is as far as possible from
' your conception of idyllic merriment. That
' delicious effervescence of the mind which we
' call fun has no equivalent for the northern
' peasant, except tipsy revelry; the only realm
' of fancy and imagination for the English
' clown exists at the bottom of the third
' quart-pot.'

This passage certainly shows observation,
but for all one can tell it may merely be the
scientific observation of the psychologist, not
the sympathetic reproduction of the artist.
As yet it lacks the concretising touch.
Similarly, when the writer goes on to remark,
' It is quite true that a thresher is likely to
' be innocent of any adroit arithmetical cheat-
' ing, but he is not the less likely to carry
' home his master's corn in his shoes and
' pocket,' we have no warranty that this could
be expanded into the Ben Tholoway of *Adam
Bede*. And even when George Eliot notices
the custom of distinguishing cousins by refer-

ring them to their father's name, we cannot de-
duce the figure of Timothy's Bess's Ben in the
same novel. Observation is, indeed, needed
for the novel, but some kinds of observation
are destructive of all individualising. Tell a
painter to observe his hand as he paints and
the result will be disastrous. Similarly, if a
writer consciously notices the processes which
make up his creations, they are doomed as
artistic presentations. Observation must have
become unconscious and ingrained in the
artist's mind before it can aid in giving the
realistic details of the novel.

And further, the novelist requires something more than keen observation of the
workings of human nature; this is useless
without the power and the love of story-tell-
ing. Nothing in these essays, nothing in the
impression George Eliot made on her friends,
indicated her possession of the faculty that
builds up incident and character into a story.
To the last she was somewhat deficient in
this, as is shown by the fact that she displays
none of the worker's joy in her own production. To tell a story requires that one should
have lived a story. And it was probably the
exceptional nature of her relations with
George Henry Lewes, which commenced in
1854, that brought about the change in
George Eliot which we have been attempting

to point out. Without going into the merits of the case, for which there are at present no trustworthy data, it is clear that to George Eliot the anti-social attitude which circumstances caused her to take up brought a complete revolution in her whole moral being, which was shaken to the depths. The modern novel is one of problem, not of action, and her own problematic position rendered her the more sensitive to the artistic side of this form of the novel.

These remarks may serve to illustrate a remarkable passage in the same essay from which the previous quotations were taken. George Eliot's theory of the function of the novel is there given, as well as her view of Dickens's art, which was developed by George Henry Lewes in the *Fortnightly Review* after Dickens's death. The whole passage deserves quotation :—

'The greatest benefit we owe to the artist, ' whether painter, poet, or novelist, is the ex- ' tension of our sympathies. Appeals founded ' on generalisations and statistics require a ' sympathy ready-made, a moral sentiment ' already in activity ; but a picture of human ' life such as a great artist can give surprises ' even the trivial and the selfish into that ' attention to what is apart from themselves, ' which may be called the raw material of

'moral sentiment. When Scott takes us into
'Luckie Mucklebackit's cottage, or tells the
'story of *The Two Drovers*,—when Words-
'worth sings to us the reverie of *Poor Susan*,—
'when Kingsley shows us Alton Locke gazing
'yearningly over the gate which leads from
'the highway into the first wood he ever saw,
'—when Hornung paints a group of chimney-
'sweepers,—more is done towards linking the
'higher classes with the lower, towards ob-
'literating the vulgarity of exclusiveness, than
'by hundreds of sermons and philosophical
'dissertations. Art is the nearest thing to
'life; it is a mode of amplifying experience
'and extending our contact with our fellow-
'men beyond the bounds of our personal lot.
'All the more sacred is the task of the artist
'when he undertakes to paint the life of the
'People. Falsification here is far more per-
'nicious than in the more artificial aspects of
'life. It is not so very serious that we should
'have false ideas about evanescent fashions
'—about the manners and conversations of
'beaux and duchesses; but it *is* serious that
'our sympathy with the perennial joys and
'struggles, the toil, the tragedy, and the
'humour in the life of our more heavily laden
'fellow-men, should be perverted, and turned
'towards a false object instead of the true one.
'This perversion is not the less fatal because

' the misrepresentation which gives rise to it
' has what the artist considers a moral end.
' The thing for mankind to know is, not what
' are the motives and influences which the
' moralist thinks *ought* to act on the labourer
' or the artisan, but what are the motives and
' influences which *do* act on him. We want
' to be taught to feel, not for the heroic artisan
' or the sentimental peasant, but for the
' peasant in all his coarse apathy, and the
' artisan in all his suspicious selfishness. We
' have one great novelist who is gifted with
' the utmost power of rendering the external
' traits of our town population; and if he
' could give us their psychological character—
' their conceptions of life, and their emotions
' —with the same truth as their idiom and
' manners, his books would be the greatest
' contribution Art has ever made to the
' awakening of social sympathies. But while
' he can copy Mrs. Plornish's colloquial style
' with the delicate accuracy of a sun-picture,
' while there is the same startling inspiration
' in his description of the gestures and phrases
' of "Boots," as in the speeches of Shake-
' speare's mobs or numskulls, he scarcely ever
' passes from the humorous and external to
' the emotional and tragic, without becoming
' as transcendent in his unreality as he was a
' moment before in his artistic truthfulness.

' But **for the** precious salt **of** his humour,
' which **compels** him **to reproduce** external
' traits that serve, in some degree, **as a cor-**
' rective **to** his frequently false psychology, **his**
' preternaturally virtuous poor children **and**
' artisans, his melodramatic boatmen **and**
' courtesans, would **be as noxious** as Eugène
' Sue's idealised proletaires in encouraging the
' miserable **fallacy that high** morality and **re-**
' fined sentiment can **grow out of harsh social**
' relations, ignorance, **and want ;** or that **the**
' working classes are **in a** condition **to** enter
' at once into **a** millennial state of *altruism,*
' wherein every one is caring **for every one**
' else, and no one for himself.'

The frequent reference **to** psychology in
this passage is significant, and indicates the
dangerous tendency **in** George Eliot's **own** art
which led to the psychological strain in *Middle-*
march **and** *Daniel Deronda,* and finally resulted
in **the** psychological **scarecrows** of *Theo-*
phrastus Such. **To the novelist 'the curtain**
is the picture,' and **if he turns to the** psychologist to analyse the painting, **only the canvas**
and frame remain **intact. There is too great**
a tendency for the psychological novelist to
regard his characters as so many *corpora vilia*
for his scientific theories. Luckily for **George**
Eliot her interests were ethical rather than
psychological, and if she ever does violence to

art, it is in the interest of morality rather than of science.

And this leads us to discuss for a moment the need of culture for the novelist. Obviously intellectual training is not alone sufficient. George Henry Lewes was exactly on a par with George Eliot in this regard, yet his *Ranthorpe* was deservedly a failure. Nor is culture combined with observation a complete equipment for the novelist. Riehl is allowed by George Eliot herself to have had a complete knowledge of the German peasant, and was besides a man of great culture ; yet his *Culturgeschichtliche Novellen,* though republished by the Pitt Press, can scarcely rank as classic. On the other hand, Auerbach and George Eliot show that wide culture is no necessary bar to sympathetic delineation of the life furthest removed from culture. In so far as culture is real and has become instinctive and unconscious, it undoubtedly tends to give a wider background to the artistic picture and to affect us at more various points of contact. But observation, psychology, and culture can only increase the artistic value of the novel in so far as they are unconsciously applied and subordinated to the interest of character and incident. The selective principle with regard to the latter cannot be of an intellectual, conscious kind at all : it must clearly be

of an **emotional** nature **akin to the** moral
faculty.

It is at this point that we touch the **secret**
spring of George Eliot's art : her whole work
is imbued with ethical notions. The novel is,
no less than the poem, a criticism of life ; and
the remarkable influence **of George** Eliot's
novels has **been mainly** due to **the** consistent
application of moral ideas to the problems set
by each novel. Their stimulative effect **was**
due to the fact that her ethical views **were in**
consonance with some of the most advanced
ideas of the age. The three chief principles
which dominated her thinking were the reign
of law in human affairs, the solidarity **of**
society, and the constitution of society as
incarnate history (the phrase is Riehl's).
Flowing from these were the ethical **laws**
which rule **the** world **of her** novels, the
principle summed up **in** Novalis's words,
' Character **is** Fate,' the radiation of good
and evil deeds **throughout society,** and the
supreme claims of family or race. Add **to**
these the scientific tone of impartiality, with
its moral analogue, the extension of sympathy
to all, and we have exhausted the *idées mères*
of George Eliot's ethical system, which differ-
entiates her novels from **all** others of the age.

These general remarks on George Eliot's
art have been suggested by **the** essay on

Riehl's studies of the natural history of German life, in which the author gives at once her theory of the function of the novelist and her general agreement with Riehl on the psychology of the peasants who were to form the main subjects of her novels. Other essays in this volume are similarly interesting, owing to the light they throw on her religious views. Two of them—on the poet Young and on Dr. Cumming—deal with the chief moral defects she had found in the religion in which she had been brought up. In the former she deals with the Divine Policeman theory of virtue, which was so favoured by Voltaire and was the chief argument formerly used to defend the immortality of the soul. It is impossible to mistake the personal tone of the following protest against this theory :—

'We can imagine the man who "denies his
' soul immortal" replying, "It is quite possible
' that *you* would be a knave, and love yourself
' alone, if it were not for your belief in immor-
' tality ; but you are not to force upon me
' what would result from your own utter want
' of moral emotion. I am just and honest, not
' because I expect to live in another world,
' but because, having felt the pain of injustice
' and dishonesty towards myself, I have a
' fellow-feeling with other men, who would
' suffer the same pain if I were unjust or dis-

' honest towards them. **Why should I** give
' my neighbour short weight in this world,
' because there is not another world in which
' **I should** have nothing to weigh out to him ?
' **I am** honest because I don't like to inflict
' evil on others in this life, not because I 'm
' **afraid of** evil to myself in another. The fact
' is, I do *not* love myself alone, whatever logi-
' cal necessity there may be for that conclusion
' in your mind. **I** have a tender love for my
' wife, and children, and friends, and through
' that love I sympathise with like affections **in**
' other men. It is a pang to me to witness
' the suffering of a fellow-being, and I feel his
' suffering the more acutely because he is
' *mortal*—because his life is so short, and I
' would have it, if possible, filled with happi-
' ness **and** not misery. Through my union
' **and** fellowship with the men and women I
' *have* **seen, I** feel **a** like, though **a** fainter,
' sympathy with those **I have** *not* seen ; and I
' am **able so to live in imagination with the**
' generations to come that their good is not
' alien to me, and is a stimulus to me to labour
' for ends which may not benefit myself, but
' **will** benefit them. It **is** possible that you
' **might** prefer to 'live the brute,' to sell
' **your country, or** to slay your father, if
' **you were not afraid** of some disagreeable
' consequences from the criminal laws of
' **another** world; **but even if I could** con-

' ceive no motive but by my own worldly
' interest or the gratification of my animal
' desires, I have not observed that beastliness,
' treachery, and parricide are the direct way
' to happiness and comfort on earth." '

Again, in the scathing review of Dr. Cumming's sermons, George Eliot protests with equal energy against the older Evangelical teaching that all virtue is useless unless done *ad majorem Dei gloriam* (p. 192). We thus see that it was disagreement with the ethical foundations of the current theology of her time which caused her revolt from it. Again, the chief interest of a somewhat unsympathetic review of Mr. Lecky's *History of Rationalism* consists in a passage at the end, in which she calls attention to ' the supremely important fact ' that science had brought about a conception of the orderly action of law on human nature, a conception which, as has been seen, dominated her whole thought.

The only paper of purely literary interest in this volume is one on Heine, which is for the most part made up of translations of autobiographic fragments. It contains, indeed, an elaborate contrast of wit and humour, which is hardly more successful than the many other attempts in the same direction, and an antithesis of French wit and German humour, which is merely an expansion of a popular prejudice.

One fine illustration redeems the essay, however; George Eliot gives as a specimen of a
Heinesque lyric Wordsworth's *She dwelt among
the untrodden ways*, the last line of which is
exactly in the manner of Heine. For the rest
one is surprised at the very ordinary and external character of her criticism. Her mind
was clearly constructive, not critical, and it is
a fundamental error to suppose that her genius
was analytical.

An *Address to Working Men*, by Felix Holt,
and an account of a three-months' stay at
Weimar complete the essays. The former re-
peats at some length the political harangues
in the novel. When Mr. Lowe said, 'Come,
let us educate our new masters,' George Eliot,
in the character of a working man, said,
'Come, let us educate ourselves.' Her intensely conservative feeling comes out strongly
in her appeals for the preservation of social
order; the notion that society is incarnate
history was sufficient to condemn with her
any sudden alteration in social relations. The
chief point of practical advice in the address
is, however, the recognition of the need of
culture and opportunities for culture by the
masses. Of the account of Weimar it is sufficient to say that it might have been written
by any English lady of education.

Attached to these essays are a few *Leaves*

from a Note-Book that might **very well have been omitted.** They are of **the period and** the type **of** *Theophrastus Such,* **and** their style is of the same harsh character, as may be **judged** by the opening sentence :—

' **To lay down** in the shape **of** practical moral
' rules courses of conduct only to be made real
' by the rarest states of motive and disposi-
' tion, tends not to elevate **but** to degrade the
' general standard, by turning that rare **attain-**
' ment from an object of admiration into **an**
' impossible prescription, against which **the**
' average **nature** first **rebels and** then flings
' **out ridicule.'**

Of course a mind **of the power of** George Eliot's could not **have been** occupied with such varied subjects without hitting upon some novel points of view or felicitous phrases. **Of** the latter we may pick out the reference of Young's faults to **a** 'pedagogic fallacy,' akin to Mr. Ruskin's 'pathetic fallacy.' **Again,** the following points are well **put** :—

' Virtue, with Young, must always squint—
' must never look straight towards the im-
' mediate object of **its emotion** and effort.
' Thus, **if** a man risks perishing in the snow
' himself rather than **forsake a** weaker com-
' rade, he must either **do this** because his
' hopes **and** fears are directed to another
' **world, or** because he desires to applaud

' himself afterwards ! Young, **if we may be-**
' lieve him, would despise the **action as folly,**
' **unless it had** these motives. **Let** us hope
' **he was** not **so bad as he** pretended **to be !**
' **The tides** of the divine life in man move
' under the thickest **ice of** theory.'

'**Love** does not **say, "I** ought to love "—
' it loves. **Pity does not** say, **" It is** right **to**
' be pitiful "—it pities. Justice **does** not say,
' **"I** am **bound to** be just "—it feels justly.
' **It is** only where moral emotion **is compara-**
' tively weak that the contemplation of **a rule**
' **or** theory habitually mingles with its action ;
' **and** in accordance with this, we think **ex-**
' perience, both in literature and life, has
' shown that the minds which are predomi-
' nantly didactic are deficient in sympathetic
' emotion. **A** man who is perpetually thinking
' in **monitory** apophthegms, who has an unin-
' termittent **flux** of rebuke, can have little
' energy left for simple feeling.'

' The deepest **curse of wrong-doing,** whether
' of the foolish **or** wicked **sort,** is **that** its
' effects are difficult **to be undone. I suppose**
' there is hardly anything more **to be shud-**
' dered at than **that** part of the history **of**
' disease which shows how, **when a man in-**
' **jures** his constitution by **a life of vicious**
' **excess, his** children and grandchildren inherit
' diseased bodies **and minds, and** how **the**

' effects of that unhappy inheritance continue
' to spread beyond our calculation. This is
' only one example of the law by which human
' lives are linked together: another example
' of what we complain of when we point to
' our pauperism, to the brutal ignorance of
' multitudes among our fellow-countrymen, to
' the weight of taxation laid on us by blame-
' able wars, to the wasteful channels made
' for the public money, to the expense and
' trouble of getting justice, and call these the
' effects of bad rule. This is the law that
' we all bear the yoke of, the law of no man's
' making, and which no man can undo.'

But such passages are few and far between,
and the general impression is left, how much
the hack-work of genius resembles that of
ordinary mortals. And though not all signs
of genius are wanting, these articles are
essentially unfinished studies and give no
foreshadowing of the finished product. Their
interest is purely relative to the light they
throw on George Eliot's mental development.

CROSS'S 'LIFE'*

THESE long-expected volumes have been compiled with great tact. Mr. Cross has aimed at making them a self revelation of his wife's career and **character**, and he has been for the most **part** successful **in the** discharge of this difficult undertaking. Some slight confusion may be at times caused by the uninterrupted printing **of** extracts of diverse tone, date, and subject; this might have been obviated by judicious 'spacing' between the successive entries. There are obviously many omissions, and some of the materials already utilised in Miss Blind's little book would have borne repetition. At times, **too, the** reader may feel the need of comment or illustration, while the continental descriptions might have been curtailed. But, these slight deductions made, **the** book is remarkably satisfactory in tone, and is especially noteworthy for a rigid abstinence from anything that could pander to mere curiosity.

* *George Eliot's Life, as related in her Letters and Journals.* Arranged and edited by her Husband, J. W. Cross. 3 vols. (Blackwood & Sons.)

D

The novel method of extracts arranged in
order of time tells the tale spontaneously, and
George Eliot the woman stands forth revealed
to the world in all the strength and refinement of her intellect, in all the clinging
trustfulness of her moral and emotional nature.
And as regards George Eliot the writer we
learn as much as it is needful to know about
the motives and processes of her art and the
outward circumstances of her activity as author.
The interest of the work naturally divides
into the personal and the artistic sides of her
life.   By a kind of coincidence these are
chiefly represented in the first and third
volumes respectively, while the intermediate
one is a sort of glorified Baedeker, giving
George Eliot's impressions of her foreign
travels between 1860 and 1870.   The modern
interest in development causes us in the first
instance to concentrate our attention on the
first volume, dealing with the life up to the
production of the first book, *Scenes of Clerical
Life*, including the difficult problem of her
relations with George Henry Lewes.   We see
there a drama of religious development which
is peculiarly significant, a display of intellectual precocity and progress, and, above all,
a peculiarly sensitive affectionateness, which
rules throughout the life and forms its most
distinctive as well as most novel feature.

The peculiarity of the religious development which strikes one most prominently in reading the earlier letters is that, in advancing towards wider views than her earlier Calvinism, George Eliot still found objects for the religious emotion that moved her so strongly in her young days. She 'found religion,' as the ascetics say, in the later forms of her belief as in the earlier, and consecrated her life to the highest and the best equally in the days of Comtism and of Calvinism. This predominantly religious tone gives an emotional unity to her life which might be easily missed, but is really the key to its various seeming fluctuations. Beginning with the conventional expressions of self-conscious humility, 'Oh that 'I might be made as useful in my lowly and 'obscure station !' (i. 43) it is seen throughout life in her high ideal of her artistic mission, and finds a final utterance in her characteristic hymn, 'O may I join the choir invisible !' Even in the first revulsion from the old faith she felt the connection between that and the new, as the following passage shows :—

'For my part, I wish to be among the 'ranks of that glorious crusade that is seeking 'to set Truth's Holy Sepulchre free from a 'usurped domination. We shall then see her 'resurrection ! Meanwhile, although I cannot

' rank among my principles of action a fear of
' vengeance eternal, gratitude for predestined
' salvation, or a revelation of future glories as
' a reward, I fully participate in the belief
' that the only heaven here, or hereafter, is
' to be found in conformity with the will of
' the Supreme; a continual aiming at the at-
' tainment of the perfect ideal, the true *logos*
' that dwells in the bosom of the one Father.'
And in a very remarkable essay on conformity
and compromise, written when she was only
twenty-three, the reason of the connection is
fully grasped and explained :—

'Agreement between intellects seems un-
' attainable, and we turn to the *truth of feeling*
' as the only universal bond of union. We
' find that the intellectual errors which we
' once fancied were a mere incrustation have
' grown into the living body, and that we
' cannot in the majority of cases wrench them
' away without destroying vitality. We begin
' to find that with individuals, as with nations,
' the only safe revolution is one arising out of
' the wants which their own progress has
' generated. It is the quackery of infidelity
' to suppose that it has a nostrum for all
' mankind, and to say to all and singular,
' "Swallow my opinions and you shall be
' whole." If, then, we are debarred by such
' considerations from trying to reorganise

'opinions, are we to remain aloof from our
'fellow-creatures on occasions when we may
'fully sympathise with the feelings exercised,
'although our own have been melted into
'another mould? Ought we not on every
'opportunity to seek to have our feelings in
'harmony, though not in union, with those
'who are often richer in the fruits of faith,
'though not in reason, than ourselves?'

One thing is clear and instructive. The
transition, brought about in the main by the
Hennells, took a grievous weight from off her
spirits. Whereas before the change we find
her saying, 'I am aweary, aweary—longing
for rest,' and speaking of herself as 'alone
in the world,' so soon as the change comes,
'I can rejoice,' she says, 'in all the joys of
humanity'; and she soon speaks of the duty
of finding happiness and of learning how to
be happy in a most satisfactory way. She is
speaking from experience when in 1847 she
suggests as a subject she should like to work
out, 'the superiority of the consolations of philo-
'sophy to those of (so-called) religion.' It is
curious to contrast all this with the totally
dissimilar behaviour of Carlyle, who became
the more morose the more widely he departed
from ancestral faith. And there is plenty of
evidence in these volumes that George Eliot's
bodily sufferings began as early and were

probably as acute as Carlyle's. Before she is
nineteen we hear of sick-headaches, and these
follow any unusual exertion throughout life.
Her gentle heroism under this infliction contrasts favourably with Carlyle's apostrophes
to gods and men on the ills of dyspepsia.

Of equal interest is it in this first volume
to follow the rapid growth of George Eliot's
intellectual power. Very few details are
given here of the actual character of her
studies in early days. But here and there
her thirst for knowledge makes itself seen
even in the days of Calvinistic strictness. At
times we catch glimpses of the artistic pre-
paration. A world of her own creation is
referred to opprobriously, and her imagination
is her enemy in the days when all fiction was
pernicious, as is stated in one of the first
letters to Miss Lewis—an amusing bit of irony,
in the old Greek sense. Very soon the tendency to scientific illustration comes, and the
following passage shows the power of description as early as 1841 :—

‘ The birds are consulting about their migra-
‘ tions, the trees are putting on the hectic or
‘ the pallid hues of decay, and begin to strew
‘ the ground, that one's very footsteps may
‘ not disturb the repose of earth and air,
‘ while they give us a scent that is a perfect
‘ anodyne to the restless spirit.’

And somewhat later there is a fine passage
descriptive of fireworks seen on the Lake of
Geneva, with 'the pale moon looking at it
all with a sort of grave surprise.' We may
notice the strain of ethical reflection so characteristic of the novels in the recognition of
the purgative effect of war, in the maxim,
'Live and teach,' proposed as a substitute for
the proverbial 'Live and learn,' in her estimate of trouble as being a deepened gaze into
life. Among the chief intellectual influences
before her father's death in 1849, which formed
the first great crisis in her life, we can trace
George Sand, Carlyle, Rousseau, and Spinoza,
and, above all, the converse with the Hennells
and the work at Strauss which resulted from
this. But perhaps the chief impression of
power is left by a few brief but weighty
remarks on the men she came in contact
with, even before she left the provincial circles.
George Dawson she estimates at once as 'not
a great man,' whereas Emerson is appreciated
as the first *man* she had known. The same
with men known through their writings.
Disraeli has 'good veins, as Bacon would
say, but there is not enough blood in them.'
Hannah More was that most disagreeable of
all monsters, a blue-stocking. Somewhat later,
when on the *Westminster* staff, she rated J. S.
Mill at something more nearly his true value

than most **of** her contemporaries, and was among the first to welcome the promise of Mr. Herbert Spencer. Of all the chief gifts of intellect displayed in her works we find adumbrations before she left Coventry. We miss, however, every indication of wit or humour till the life of the capitals is reached in Geneva and London. The spirit of **ob**-servation becomes self-conscious, and Lewes is hit off as a 'sort of miniature Mirabeau,' Alboni as '**a** very fat siren,' Combe as 'an apostle with a front and back drawing-room.' Leroux 'disagrees with all but Pierre Leroux.' In short, we have all the indications of George Eliot the novel-writer except the novels. And even about these there is a remarkable quotation from a letter of Mrs. Bray to her sister on September 25th, 1846, exactly ten years before *Amos Barton*: 'Miss Evans looks very ' brilliant just now. We fancy she must be ' writing her novel.' Yet this must have only been an *Ahnung*—as Mr. Cross is fond of saying —for no people were more surprised at the revelation of George Eliot's abilities as a novelist than the Brays a **dozen** years after.

Her relation to the Brays is in many re-spects decisive and typical. We come to the secret recesses of her being, to the key of all that is problematic in her career and character, when **we** encounter the remarkable union of hard-headed intellect and impetuous affection, such as we see in her letters to the Brays. Nor does this die away with youth: the same gushing tone—there is no other word for it— is kept up with Miss Hennell to the last, and is even adopted with friends gained in the decline of life. This stern independence of intellect combined with a complete depend- ence on others for the emotional life, gives the characteristic tone throughout her life, and we are continually coming across a severe philosophical disquisition side by side with an outburst of uncontrollable affection or longing. She has doubtless portrayed this side of her nature in Maggie Tulliver with her impulsive affection, her emotional dependence on others. But she had recognised it much earlier when speaking of herself as 'ivy-like as I am by nature,' and in this peculiarly womanly quality she remained a very woman to the last. Manly intellect and girlish heart were united in her to an unusual degree.

This problematic nature serves to explain —so far as it bears explanation—the crux of her life—her union with George Henry Lewes. Mr. Cross, with much tact and wisdom, refuses to discuss the question. The only contribu- tion he gives to its solution is a letter addressed to Mrs. Bray a year after the 'union' was entered upon. Here the question is made to turn on a difference of opinion as to the marriage laws, and George Eliot's only defence, if any, is that she has not entered on 'light and easily broken ties.' But as a matter of fact she would have herself owned that this was no defence against setting herself at variance with the moral instincts of all whom she held dear. It is true that six years before she had said, *à propos* of *Jane Eyre* :—

'All self-sacrifice is good, but one would 'like it to be in a somewhat nobler cause 'than that of a diabolical law which chains a 'man soul and body to a putrefying carcass.'

But that would be at best an excuse for Lewes, not for herself. As a matter of fact there was no excuse, and in a very significant letter to Mrs. Taylor she practically surrenders any pleas as regards the iniquity of the marriage laws, and desires the legal title she should theoretically have despised :—

'For the last six years I have ceased to 'be "Miss Evans" for any one who has 'personal relations with me — having held 'myself under all the responsibilities of a 'married woman. I wish this to be distinctly 'understood; and when I tell you that we 'have a great boy of eighteen at home who 'calls me "mother," as well as two other 'boys, almost as tall, who write to me under 'the same name, you will understand that the

' point is not one of mere egoism or personal
' dignity, when I request that any one who
' has a regard for me will cease to speak of
' me by my maiden name.'

In reality, however, the clue to her conduct
is to be sought in the girlish impulsiveness of
her affectionate nature, which seems so hard
to connect with her accuracy and independence
of thought. She speaks of Lewes having
' quite won my liking in spite of myself' a
year before their flight, and her hurried letter
to the Brays at the last moment shows that
the momentous decision was the work of impulse. She had evidently found in him some
one to cling to amid the dreary solitude of
life in London lodgings, and Lewes took the
responsibility of accepting her sacrifice.

In justice to Lewes it must be remembered
that he could have had no idea of the transcendent nature of the woman whose life he
was accepting. Mr. F. W. Myers tells a story
of some impudent ass who wrote to George
Eliot after *Middlemarch* condoling with her
for being mated to a Casaubon. There would
have been less incongruity if Lewes had been
compared to Ladislaw, who was, one feels,
almost equally unworthy of Dorothea. Lewes
is gradually being rated at his true worth : a
philosopher among journalists, a journalist
among philosophers, he has left behind him

nothing that will live, not even the overrated *Life of Goethe,* the critical portions of which are very thin.   But George Eliot was herself one of the first to protest against the habit of mind which requires equality of gifts in husband and wife, and we cannot hope that every Elizabeth Barrett will find her Robert Browning.

And it must be owned that, once the lapse committed, Lewes did all in his power to keep at a distance every bad influence   He encouraged her first writing, and checked by his vivacity the tendency to over-seriousness which came to her with the knowledge of her powers and responsibilities.   All the petty details of life were warded off from her by Lewes with watchful care.   The somewhat unreasoning sensibility to adverse criticism was carefully considered by Lewes, who acted as her private secretary.   And all this was effected through long years often filled with illness of his own.   He may have encouraged in later years the psychological strain of her work to its detriment, and whatever glimpses we have of his critical influence in early years seem by no means fortunate : it was through him, *e.g.,* that Dinah was made to marry Adam Bede.

And, above all, the lapse must be forgiven or forgotten which led to that fusion of the

intellect and **the** emotions necessary to the
artistic impulse. Everything seems to show
that George Eliot's memories **of her home**
life would have slumbered **for ever but for**
this moral crisis in her own life, which stirred
her to the depths of her being and withdrew
her from **the** conventions of society. There
is not the slightest indication throughout the
biography, except **the** chance shot of Mrs.
Bray mentioned above, which could lead **her**
friends to imagine any other future for George
Eliot than one similar to that **of** her friend
Miss Sara Hennell. Her attitude of moral
defiance to the world threw her back on the
resources of her own life and gave birth to the
peculiarities of her art. What those peculiarities are, and the light thrown upon them
by the book before us, must **now** demand
our attention.

The problem **of George** Eliot's life is **to**
explain **how a** mind **of** so eminently a speculative **turn** should have shown the artistic
impulse for creation **so** late in life and should
have succeeded so eminently. The characteristics of her art show us the reverse of this
difficulty. We have to reconcile her distinct
power of realising her characters with her
equally marked capacity for what we may
term moralising them. A well-known example will illustrate the union, in this case

the fusion, of the two modes of work.   In the catastrophe of *The Mill on the Floss* the novelist describes the mass of broken timber bearing down upon the brother and sister (physicists say the boat would always keep ahead).   Tom sees it, cries, 'It is coming, Maggie!' clasps her, and they meet their fate. For the artist who only wished to realise the scene this would suffice.   But with George Eliot there is the equal need to 'moralise' it, and so she continues: 'The boat reappeared ' —but brother and sister had gone down in an ' embrace never to be parted: living through ' again in one supreme moment the days when ' they had clasped their little hands in love and ' roamed the daisied fields together.'   The beauty of this passage must not blind us to its inartistic, or rather extra-artistic, character. The emotions, æsthetic or moral, which the artist desired to produce by this reference to childhood's days ought to have been produced spontaneously by the catastrophe itself if the previous presentation of their childhood had been artistically effective.   But it is George Eliot's peculiarity that she tries to bring into consciousness those feelings which her narrative ought to have produced by itself.   She makes two attempts to produce her effect— by artistic presentation and by philosophic reflection.   By so endeavouring she practically

confesses the failure of her art to do its work
unaided. But much of that failure consists in
the nature of the work which she wished to
do with her novels.

Before she had written any work of imagination, Lewes expressed his doubts whether
she had the power of dramatic presentation,
though she might have 'wit, description, and
philosophy.' As it turned out, she possessed
the power of dramatic presentation in a very
high degree ; the breakfast at which Arthur
Donnithorne did *not* confess to Parson Irwine,
the last meeting between Dorothea and
Rosamund, Tulliver's inscription in the family
Bible, the appearance of Silas Marner at the
Rainbow, Klesmer's visit to the Meyricks, may
be instanced as examples of this. But the
power of imaginative presentation, though it
must have always existed, came to her late in
life. It was most probably aroused by the
attitude of moral defiance toward the world
which her relations to Lewes had brought
about. But there is also evidence in these
volumes that the process of artistic assimila-
tion was with her unusually slow, as she recognised in an interesting letter to Madame
Bodichon :—

' I do wish much to see more of human life
' —how can one see enough in the short years
' one has to stay in the world ? But I meant

' that at present my mind works with the
' most freedom and the keenest sense of poetry
' in my remotest past, and there are many strata
' to be worked through before I can begin to
' use, *artistically*, any material I may gather in
' the present. Curiously enough, *à propos* of
' your remark about *Adam Bede*, there is much
' less " out of my own life " in that book—*i.e.*
' the materials are much more a combination
' from imperfectly-known and widely-sundered
' elements than the *Clerical Scenes*.'

But while her imagination was thus ruminat-
ing, as it were, her whole spiritual life was
taken up with an entirely different order of
interests. Beginning with that thirst of
knowledge for its own sake which goes to
make the great scholar, it was soon diverted
into the two chief channels of intellectual interest which characterised her age—the decay
of the older religious ideals and the growth
of a scientific conception of the universe, including man. And with her these two branches
of speculation were reconciled by her recognition of the facts of human emotion underlying
both. The following passage from an instructive note on *The Spanish Gypsy*, unfortunately
too long to quote in its entirety, puts the germ
of George Eliot's reconciliation of religion and
science :—

'There is really no moral " sanction " but

' this inward impulse.   The will of God is
' the same thing as the will of other men, com-
' pelling us to work and avoid what they have
' seen to be harmful to social existence.   Dis
' joined from any perceived good, the divine
' will is simply so much as we have ascer-
' tained of the facts of existence which com-
' pel obedience at our peril.'

These facts which compel obedience are
declared to be ' the part which is played in
' the general human lot by hereditary condi-
' tions in the largest sense and the fact that
' what we call duty is entirely made up of such
' conditions.' The scientific conception of law
in human nature was combined by her with
the moral or religious fact of duty.   Besides
this the Comtist view of society as an organism
was translated into the ethical consideration of
the radiation of good and evil deeds throughout society.   The moral progress of the world
would depend, according to her, upon the
degree in which men's minds were trained to
see the consequences of their egoistic impulses.
In an interesting correspondence with the Hon.
Mrs. Ponsonby, where she sharply distinguishes
her theory from the physical Positivism of
Professor Tyndall and others, she clearly
puts this aspiration :—

' With regard to the pains and limitations of
' one's personal lot, I suppose there is not a

E

' single man, or woman, who has not more or less
' need of that stoical **resignation which** is often
' a hidden heroism, or who, in considering his
' or her past history, is not aware that it has
' been cruelly affected by the ignorant or selfish
' action of some fellow-being in a more or less
' close relation of life. And **to** my mind,
' there can be no stronger motive, than this
' perception, to an energetic effort that the
' lives nearest to us shall not suffer in a like
' manner from *us*.'

It is impossible to say with what success she
would have handled **these views in** the connected exposition of **a** philosophical work. As
all the world now knows, she chose **to** expound
them in the form of fiction, and determined to
make the novel what history is said to be—
philosophy teaching by example. At first she
was not conscious of any such aim. When the
Scenes were completed she felt only ' a deep
' satisfaction in having done a piece of faithful
' work that will perhaps remain like a primrose
' root in the hedgerow and gladden and chasten
' human hearts in years to come.' Nor is there
any hint of conscious **motive** in *Adam Bede*
and *The Mill on the Floss,* her **two** greatest
works. But immediately after the great success of *Adam Bede* the sense of her responsibilities settled upon her with only too
heavy pressure. She feels it her ' vocation **to**

speak to one's fellow-men ' and make her work
' an instrument of culture.' And henceforward
this motive was conscious with her, and in each
of her creations she looks round for some idea
which the fiction shall embody. The process
begins with *Silas Marner,* which grew from ' the
merest millet-seed of *thought.'* Of this she
says : ' It sets—or is intended to set—in a
' strong light the remedial influences of pure,
' natural human relations.' And in *Silas Marner*
the balance between artistic creation and
philosophic construction is most evenly held
of all her books, of which it is in a way the
quintessence. Henceforth, however, the philosophic interest is predominant, and her words
are intended more to point a moral than to
adorn a tale. *Romola* has its moral summed
up in the last words of the book, and in an
elaborate letter to Mr. R. H. Hutton she avows
her intention of expressing certain truths
by the relations of Baldo and Baldassare, of
Tito and his patrons, and seems to be chiefly
interested in Romola herself as presenting a
moral problem. The elaborate note on *The
Spanish Gypsy* before referred to gives the *motif*
of the work as the clashing of individual desires
and hereditary claims. *Middlemarch,* as its
Proem states, is a contribution towards the
woman question, though its scale happily
caused it to overflow into a study of provincial

life. *Deronda* was intended to ennoble Judaism in the estimation of Christians and of Jews, and it would almost seem from a letter to Professor Kaufmann, couched in extravagant terms, that the only object in introducing Grandcourt and Gwendolen was to contrast Christian society with Jewish family life, to the disadvantage of the former. In all these later works the novel in George Eliot's hand had become the *Tendenz-roman,* not alone the philosophic novel, as Mr. Shorthouse, for example, conceives it, but philosophy in the form of the novel.

It is not our intention to discuss here the artistic value of the *Tendenz-roman.* The function of criticism is to classify and analyse much more than to judge. Its artistic limitations are obvious : with the whole field of life before it, the *Tendenz-roman* has to confine itself to its *Tendenz.* Its artistic value is dependent in large measure on its philosophic truth. The temptation to philosophise formally has its dangers, as George Eliot recognised when she wrote to Mr. Blackwood that she is in danger of refining where novel-readers only think of skipping. But the point that comes out with most fulness in this *Life* is the high function which such writing must claim for itself, 'the high responsibilities of literature that undertakes to represent life.' The following catena of passages from the book

before us will show the sacredness which
attached to George Eliot's calling as she
viewed its functions :—

' My function is that of the *æsthetic*, not the
' doctrinal teacher—the rousing of the nobler
' emotions, which make mankind desire the
' social right, not the prescribing of special
' measures, concerning which the artistic mind,
' however strongly moved by social sympathy,
' is often not the best judge. It is one thing
' to feel keenly for one's fellow-being ; another
' to say, "This step, and this alone, will be the
' best to take for the removal of particular
' calamities." '

'The things you tell me are just such as I
' need to know—I mean about the help my
' book is to the people who read it. The
' weight of my future life,—the self-question-
' ing whether my nature will be able to meet
' the heavy demands upon it, both of personal
' duty and intellectual production,—presses
' upon me almost continually in a way that
' prevents me even from tasting the quiet joy
' I might have in the *work done.*'

' I think æsthetic teaching is the highest
' of all teaching, because it deals with life in
' its highest complexity. But if it ceases to
' be purely æsthetic—if it lapses anywhere
' from the picture to the diagram—it becomes
' the most offensive of all teaching.'

This lofty sense of the sacredness of her

calling may in some measure account for the sensitiveness which she showed towards adverse criticism. When a writer is advocating a doctrine it is natural that he should be disappointed if his views are not even seen. And certainly by couching her opinions in the form of novels George Eliot did her best to withhold them from all but the most thoughtful. Hence a continual feeling—often expressed in her diary—that her efforts had been vain, a 'horrible scepticism' as to the effectiveness of her work. Lewes used to keep from her all critical notices except those that were favourable. The *Athenæum* is considered to have given 'the best literary critique' of *The Spanish Gypsy,* while, on the other hand, certain expressions in a letter to Mr. Charles Lewes show that our review of *Theophrastus Such* displeased her. And, indeed, as was but natural, she got to know of most unfavourable criticisms, notwithstanding all her contempt for 'damnatory praise from ignorant journalists.' Her answers to those criticisms are often of interest ; thus she informs one of her correspondents that there is not one thing put into Mr. Poyser's mouth that is due to memory. If so, it is curious that she should make Parson Irwine say of one of them that it is as good as a fable of Æsop. So, too, we learn that there is not a single portrait in *Adam Bede*—a statement that depends very much on the **exact** meaning to be attached to the term ' portrait.' This excessive sensibility **is** seen at its maximum intensity in connection with the imposture attempted **by** Mr. Liggins of Nuneaton. **One** would have thought that a woman possessed of such powers of humour would have been more impressed by the ridiculous than by the serious aspect of the **incident.** **But** George Eliot returns **again and** again to **the** subject in a tone of sincere annoyance.

And finally, the predominance of the philo- sophic over the artistic spirit in George Eliot has tended to make these volumes, containing the record of her private life, rather dull and— dare we say it?—commonplace. She was **a** great woman, but this is not **a** great book. Like all thinkers, she tended **to** weave a **web** of theory between herself and life, and seemed to **reserve all** her humour and liveliness **for** her books. **It is** possible that Mr. Cross has created this impression **by an** ill-judged ex- cision of anything **that does not** display **his** wife on the stilts of philosophy **and** ethics. But as he claims vivacity as one **of her** prominent qualities, it is more likely that **it** did not display itself in her letter-writing. **And** the tendency to abstract theorising has **removed from** these volumes almost all personal traits of the many distinguished **men** and women with whom George Eliot came in contact. Even the personal details of her own life had, for the most part, been discounted in the articles that appeared after her death. What we chiefly notice are some of her literary opinions and prejudices. Byron was the most vulgar-minded genius that ever lived, the *Iliad* is a semi-savage poem, *Père Goriot* a hateful book (*i.e.* has no *Tendenz*), the *Origin of Species* will not produce much effect because ill arranged, but expresses the adhesion of a well-known naturalist (this on the appearance of the book). Before the *Vie de Jésus* she felt more kinship with Renan than with any other contemporary writer, but afterwards she gives up her high estimate of Renan. At times we may see bits of the novels in the making. Overbeck at Rome clearly suggested Neumann in *Middlemarch*, Mr. Frederic Harrison seems to have suggested the *Legend of Jubal* and supplied the legal technicalities of *Felix Holt*. We may catch the origin of the opening scene of *Deronda* in the girl gambler described here (iii. 171). A sensible letter to Mrs. Beecher Stowe on spiritualism may be recommended to the notice of the Society for Psychical Research. Mr. Cross has given with admirable taste a few Boswellisms. His wife told him that *Romola* found her young and left her old. The interview between Dorothea and Rosamund was written off in a fever of excitement, and stands now as at first written. But these items of interest are few and far between, and the book as a whole might more easily be the record of a *savant* than of a literary artist. In every way the total impression is sad and sombre. And so we lay down these volumes with the impression of a life disfigured by one great lapse that overshadowed it to the end, but ennobled by high gifts devoted with self-denying thoroughness to a lofty conception of the function of the depicter of human life. The novelist's art has never been made so sacramental as by George Eliot.

MATTHEW ARNOLD

April 15, 1888

MATTHEW ARNOLD

HE terribly sudden death of Matthew Arnold has deprived England of an intellectual force of a high order. A striking and influential individuality is lost to English thought and letters. Matthew Arnold was the poet and critic of the age of transition which separates so widely the England of to-day from the England of the Reform Bill, or, to come down even later, from the England of the Great Exhibition. The changes in taste, in feeling, in the general attitude towards the fundamental problems of religion, of society, and of politics, have been enormous, and in all of them, except, perhaps, the last, Matthew Arnold has been an abiding influence. We shall never, perhaps, fully appreciate the way in which he softened the asperities of the conflicts which raged round him by his imperturbable good humour, and even by the mannerisms which diverted the stress of feeling. The solvent of his criticism was diluted to the exact strength where it

could effect its purpose while giving least pain.

He began life as a poet, and in a measure remained one always, if we can divorce the poet from the technique of his art. His was a poetic force, a uniform recognition of the permanent power and reality of the ideal element in human character. His appeal was always to that, whether he were discussing Heine or Tolstoï, Irish affairs or Board schools. So far he was a poetic force in English thought and affairs. But in things specifically poetic he touched his readers less than any other Victorian poet of the first rank. Yet he is among the masters, his diction is unrivalled for purity and dignity, he strikes his notes with no faltering hand. Why then, is he not impressive? Because his problems and his moods are not poetic problems or poetic moods. Intellectual doubt has found its voice in Matthew Arnold's most sincere utterances, and doubt can never touch a wide circle. *Obermann Once More* or *The Scholar Gypsy* will answer to some moods of some men as few poems answer to the inmost depths. But the moods are rare among men, and the appeal of the poems must be as rare. Strangely enough, while Matthew Arnold deals most powerfully with one aspect of the inward conflict, he has been almost equally

successful in the most objective form of
poems, the heroic narrative. When he was
urging with all his command of paradox that
the English hexameter—the existence of
which still remains to be proved—was the
best medium into which to translate Homer,
he himself was giving in his *Sohrab and
Rustum* the nearest analogue in English to
the rapidity of action, plainness of thought,
plainness of diction, and the nobleness of
Homer. Yet even here we felt that something was wanting, as we feel in almost all
attempts at reproduction of the Romance
temper: it is not sincere, and cannot, therefore, be great. Where Matthew Arnold is
sincere in his poetic work is when he gives
expression to his 'yearning for the light,' and
summons the spirit of renunciation to support
him through the days of gloom.

These moods he reserved for expression in
verse. In prose no one is less gloomy than
he. If we might define him as a happy
Heine, we should give the best point of view
from which to survey his prose work, his
criticism of life that underlies and involves all
his criticism of books, of faiths, and of institutions. Like the German poet, he was armed
with all the culture of his time—science does
not count in such matters—and like him he
played off the one side of his nature against

the other.   But the circumstances of his life
saved him from the bitterness of Heine,
while they intensified that tendency to good-
humoured tolerance which gave to his work
much power in some directions and robbed it
of much in others.

It is usual to speak of Matthew Arnold as
having revolutionised English criticism, by
which is usually meant book-criticism.   As a
matter of fact he did very little in the way of
'judging' books, and what he did in this way
was by no means always instructive or trustworthy.   His celebrated slip about Shelley's
letters, the selections he made from Byron,
may be recalled as instances of uncertain vision
or imperfect appreciation.   In introducing the
methods of Sainte-Beuve into England, he
transferred the interest in criticism from the
books to the man.   What he did in criticism
was to introduce the *causerie*, and with it the
personal element.   Instead of the 'we' of the
older *régime*, the critic, even if he use the
plural pronoun, professes to give no more than
the manner in which a new work strikes his
individuality.   If this method has been the
cause or occasion of much affectation in contemporary criticism, it has raised criticism into
the sphere of literary art by giving it the
personal element.   The personality of Matthew
Arnold was, with all its affectations and

mannerisms, so attractive that a *causerie* with him charmed not so much by adding to our information about the author or his book, as because it added to our knowledge of Matthew Arnold.

His criticism of books, we have said, was a criticism of life, and here his work touched the deepest problems of his time, problems social and problems theological. We all know his method of exposition. A view being taken, a phrase, more or less felicitous, is selected to express the view, and henceforth the changes are rung upon the phrase till the dullest of readers cannot fail to grasp the particular view which it was desired to impress on him. The trick of iteration, exasperating as it was, effected its purpose, and the formulæ 'sweet-' ness and light,' 'criticism of life,' 'barbarians, 'Philistines, and populace,' 'the need of ex-'pression, the need of manners, the need of 'intellect, the need of beauty, and the need 'of conduct,' have bitten the more deeply into the contemporary consciousness because they were formulæ, and could be easily re-called. This effect was mainly mechanical; not so the discussions which led up to them, were summarised in them, or were deduced from them. Therein Arnold showed his powers of social analysis, and his powers were great. His summary of 'needs' given above is a remarkable description of man as a social being. Again, the cultus of 'culture,' to which he gave the vogue, was in his hands something precise. Civilisation is a big thing to analyse or to talk about, yet we felt, when he was talking about it, that it was something real and definite that he was discussing, and not the vague abstractions of the sophist.

This power of analysis showed itself in the series of theological studies beginning with *Literature and Dogma*. As regards his own solution of the religious problem, if solution it can be called, little need here be said. His very formula, purposely vague and indefinite as it was, is its own condemnation. But it has not been sufficiently recognised how the introduction of his literary tone, his many-sidedness, and the gentle irony with which he treated all extremes helped to prevent an explosion of theological or anti-theological polemics. Mr. Morley has recently been confessing that the tone of the *Fortnightly* was needlessly aggressive. But for Matthew Arnold's intervention the struggle would have been à outrance. He brought into it the spirit of an 'honest broker,' and had effect with both parties, because each felt that he was in sympathy with its best self.

Yes, that is even so with the Philistines and the Nonconformists. Amid all his wit—or

rather because his wit was so mild and free
from caustic—the Puritan **part** of the nation
felt that he too was on the side of the angels.
He was **so** respectable, after **all.**   Herein
comes the great difference between him **and**
Heine, who was not respectable at all ; **and**
Renan, who always shows a hankering after
the **life** of *les gais.*   **But** Matthew Arnold was
intensely sensitive **and** scrupulous **in** this
regard, almost to the **point** of Podsnappery.
Therefore the British public would allow him
a hearing on the problems of life.

There was no affectation in all this.   **The**
Puritan in him came near the self-restraint of
his father's Romans, or the artistic balance of
life which he respected in the best Greeks.
He was too much at ease in Zion to **be** of the
stuff of which prophets are made, yet there
was something in him akin to the spirit of the
old prophets.   Hence it was that he was **so**
influential **with the** Philistines ; **he** was in **a**
measure of them, **though he saw their faults**
and narrownesses.   **Half** humorously **he** recognised this in **one of** his **books, and** there
can be little doubt **of** its **truth and of its**
influence.   Because he was of them, the Philis-
tines, *i.e.* Nonconformists and Low Church-
men, listened **to** him, with the result that the
Low Church is **no** more ; **and Nonconformity**
is Broad Church.

We have laid stress on the theological
activity of Arnold because its importance is
apt to be obscured by the fact that his particular way of putting his solution of theological difficulties is not likely to gain disciples.
But for all that, the discussions have had as
much effect on English theology as anything
of the past quarter of a century, and he himself was in the right in laying stress upon his
theological activity and its results as the most
influential and most abiding part of his work.

A word or two may here be added on his
general attitude towards politics. His appeal
for detachment from party politics is part of
a general tendency which seems to be dis-
severing everywhere the thinking part of the
nations from active share in the politics of the
democracy. The formation of a party of In-
dependents, advocated by Mr. Lowell in the
United States, is an instance of what we mean.
By adopting this attitude Matthew Arnold
showed less than his usual insight and sagacity.
His influence in this direction cannot be said
to have been for good.

He that is gone would not have been satisfied with any estimate of his life-work which
did not take account of his strivings for educational reform, especially as regards middle-
class schools. In English social arrangements
he saw one great blot, the separation of classes

which could be traced to school-days, and he argued, justly enough, that it would never cease till the enormous difference in the tone of boys' schools for the upper classes and of boys' schools for the middle classes was done away with. It cannot be said that his insistence on this point was effectual, though the improved tone of schools for middle-class girls may possibly be connected with it. But there can be little doubt of the brilliant suggestiveness of many of his interesting reports on education, which we trust will be now brought together in book form. Rarely have Bluebooks been made so enjoyable as those which contained Matthew Arnold's racy comments on things in general, and school things in particular.

He was a poet throughout, we have said, and he himself has defined a poet as a critic of life. Would that all poets were critics so genial! In that respect the style was the man, and no man was so charming to his intimates as Matthew Arnold. It may be suspected that when we come to know the private lives of the men of letters of this, or rather of the preceding generation, few will leave so pleasant an impression, few will seem so livable with as he. That easy temper which perhaps prevented him from giving his message in a more assured tone, or from

giving a more assured message, made him a
delightful companion. And a delightful companion he is, too, in his books, with their subacid egotisms, their easy flow of keen-sighted
analysis, their sympathy with the ideal, and,
above all, that determination to see things as
in themselves they really are, which gives
the virile strength that would otherwise be
wanting. His books and he have done their
work so well that they can never appeal to
any later age with so much force as they have
to this. But because they have had so direct
an appeal to this, they must live as typical of
our age and representative of it.

'DISCOURSES IN AMERICA'*

 VERY one will welcome another volume of *causeries* from the hand of our only English master in this branch of literature, Mr. Matthew Arnold. Notwithstanding the attempts of many would-be imitators, he alone possesses the lightness of touch, width of view, sanity of criticism, and individuality of style which are needed to give permanent value to what seems at first sight to be merely a form of the higher journalism. The combination of these qualities is rare enough to account for the influence possessed by the men in whom they occur. Mr. Matthew Arnold in England, M. Renan and M. Scherer in France, and Mr. Lowell in America, almost exhaust the list; and of all the masters of the *causerie* Mr. Matthew Arnold is in some respects the most influential in England, for reasons which may well engage our attention after we have made a few remarks on the present instalment of his work.

* *Discourses in America*. By Matthew Arnold. (Macmillan & Co.)

This consists of only three discourses—the Rede Lecture adapted to American audiences and the specially American lectures on Numbers and Emerson. With the aid of wide margins and a liberal amount of 'fat,' as the printers call it, the text is doled out in pages of but nineteen lines each, and thus the three articles are successfully expanded into a booklet of over two hundred pages. Small as it is, the volume differs favourably from some of the recent republications of Mr. Arnold's utterances in that it contains only specimens of his best work, and we may perhaps add that in it he dismounts from his over-ridden hobby—State schools for the middle classes. Each of the three essays attracted attention when first delivered—readers will remember the ludicrous blunders made by the American reporters with the goddess Lubricity in *Numbers*—and they were as eagerly read when republished in magazines. Now collected in a volume, they will be as popular as any in the series in which they are published, and have a good chance of being revived in the far distant day when their copyright shall have run out —the most practical test that occurs to us to determine whether a book really belongs to English literature.

Much comment on essays so much commented on at the time of their appearance were perhaps needless. We may remark, however, that the lecture on **literature and** science has lost somewhat in its passage across **the** Atlantic. There **was** a peculiar aptitude **in its** delivery in the Senate House at Cambridge, where everything seems **to be** telling for science rather **than** literature. **And** there **was a specially** interesting passage **in** the original, now omitted, which dealt with the difference **of** the **two** universities— Oxford the **home of** great movements, Cambridge of great men. On the general merits of the great question—literature or science as training for life—Mr. Arnold is clearly on the right side, and even Professor Huxley scarcely attempts to deny this. But it is curious that Mr. Arnold omits to notice that there is a side **of** literary work which tends to give all, or nearly all, the educational advantages claimed for science. A work like Munro's *Lucretius* is in reality **as** scientific as **Roscoe** and Schorlemmer's *Chemistry*. **In Germany** both would be included under the comprehensive 'Wissenschaft.' Observation, induction, hypothesis, verification, quantitative analysis, and even **to** some extent experiment, are all applicable **to** Homer or the 'Nibelungenlied' as **to the** triassic strata. Indeed, a good case might be made out for showing that **Mr.** Arnold, in his discourse on Numbers, is simply applying the

ordinary scientific law of error—the principle
of deviations from an average so admirably
applied in Mr. Galton's *Hereditary Genius*.
His comfortable doctrine of the remnant is in
reality based on a similar assumption, and
much of it is seen to be untrustworthy when
one remembers that the curve of error may
take different forms, and the remnant be
smaller though the numbers be larger. As a
matter of fact, is it not the universal experience that the saving remnant, even in
America, is small in proportion to the mass of
self-seeking Philistinism? And if we turn to
China or India, the doctrine of the remnant
has very little comfort left for us. Opinions,
too, might differ as to the extent to which the
worship of the goddess Aselgeia is corrupting
French culture. The success of a mediocre
master like M. Ohnet, simply because he does
not bow to the ruling goddess, is sufficient to
show the strength of the protest against the
worship of Lubricity.

Here, probably, Mr. Matthew Arnold would
agree with us, the only difference of opinion
being as to the extent of the evil. On this
it may be remarked that it has been long
existent without producing any widely apparent ill effects, and that it is in large
measure counteracted by the intense family
love of the Frenchman and the more robust

life of the provinces. But we prefer not to parade differences where there is so much with which we can agree and from which we can learn. The analysis of the French character and its threefold strain—Gallic, Latin, and Germanic—recalls some of the best parts of the *Celtic Literature*. The admirable quotations from Newman, Carlyle, Goethe, and Emerson, in the opening passage of the essay on the last, together with the remarks on each author—often but a word, but what an instructive word !—exhibit Mr. Arnold at one of his best moments; as, indeed, the whole discourse on Emerson shows him to us in one of his happiest hours of inspiration, and might be selected as giving an admirable specimen of his peculiar qualities as a critic of letters and of life ; or, as Mr. Arnold would say, it gives us his method and his secret.

There is an apt phrase—we believe, of Professor Huxley's—which exactly expresses the *differentia* of Mr. Arnold's studies : they are lay sermons. The object of the sermon may be assumed to be the moral regeneration of the hearers. This is clearly and avowedly the object of most of Mr. Arnold's utterances. Notice how he invariably picks out the favourite sin of his audience. At the Royal Institution, in the midst of the London season, he lectures on equality. At Cam-

bridge he avers that with the majority of
mankind a little of mathematics goes a long
way, and that science cannot satisfy the soul
of man.　He crosses to America, and there he
chooses as his special topic Numbers, preaching to the text, 'The majority are bad.'　For
every one will recognise that Mr. Arnold's
lectures have the note of the sermon method
in this at least, that they start from a text—
it may be from the Bible, it may be from
Menander—to which the discourse returns time
after time, with a reiteration which some may
find wearisome, but which clearly effects the
purpose of impressing itself on the method.

His method, then, is that of the lay sermon.
Would that clerical sermons were ever as
good !　His secret is his subacid reasonableness
and his serious levity or frivolous seriousness.
What strikes one in his criticisms of life even
more than their penetration is their sanity and
completeness.　Many a controversial victory
he has won in discussions about letters or life,
or sometimes even in politics, by attending to
the one question, What are the actual and
complete facts of the case ?　He takes human
nature all round, and sees how far a proposed
remedy answers to all its needs.　Herein he
is really penetrated by the scientific spirit in
its best aspect, and he has been no insufficient
teacher of the higher anthropology.　That in

part is the secret of his influence. Men see
that what he says tallies in the main with what
they know, and at the same time they are half
attracted half repelled by the tone in which
he says it. If we may so put it, he pretends
not to be serious, and by the very pretence
convinces one of his seriousness. It is, in
fact, this seriousness, the conviction his
words convey that his deepest concern is
with the things of moral import, that gives
such authority to his word among Englishmen.
The things of conduct are, after all, what both
he and they have most at heart, and they
listen to him as he discourses on things of
sweetness and light—now, alas! becoming
rarer and rarer with him—because they know
that in his hands they have intimate bearing
on conduct. Hence Mr. Matthew Arnold may
say things in a tone which would be censured
in another. There is a passage in these discourses about M. Blowitz and the Eternal
which, even in Mr. Arnold, is as near want of
taste as it is possible to go. But one knows
that Mr. Arnold, after all, is not really lacking
in reverence, and so the lapse is overlooked.
Reflecting on this, one cannot help thinking
what a force Mr. Arnold would be if he
dropped his cloak of levity. He has given a
clever sermon on Gray ; text : ' He never spoke
out.' One feels that Mr. Arnold has never

spoken out the faith that is in him. He began
life as an Hellene of the Hellenes, and was as
one of those who are at ease in Zion. He
has gradually become more Hebraic than the
Hebrews, but yet retains the easy manner of
the sons of light. What a motive force he
might be if he adapted his style to his matter !
Mr. Arnold has some admirable words on
Carlyle here in the pages before us. Carlyle
is weighed in the balance and found wanting ;
but if we may deplore the want of sweetness
in Carlyle, might we not regret its overabun-
dance in Mr. Arnold's nature ? His best friends
might wish to see him—they would certainly be curious to see him—lose his temper
for once in a way over some subject that
deserves to rouse his ire.

ROBERT BROWNING

December 12, 1889

NE by **one the** *Dii majores* **are** leaving **us :** Carlyle, George Eliot, Matthew Arnold ; and now Robert Browning, a greater name **than** all these, has passed into **silence.** It is almost startling to notice how their death radically alters their relation **to** us. Not only **is** their work rounded off, finished in a double **sense,** completed into **a** system, informed with **a new** life, as if, indeed, the poet's soul had passed at once from the body to the works. The poet has gone ; his works at **once** group themselves into an organic whole, and become his work. Yet **a** still more vital change comes over **our** relations to the imaginative creator when his bodily presence is withdrawn. He **ceases** to be ours alone ; Robert Browning **no** longer speaks **only for** and to Victorian England. **He** becomes **part of** England of the past and of the future—part of the spiritual heritage for which Englishmen **have** in the past shown themselves willing to die—part of the English ideal, towards which the best **of** Englishmen aim to live. One advantage immediately accrues from the ces-

sation of all personal intercourse between the world and the poet. The idle chatter of relative merit, 'Is he greater than A?' 'Is he better than B?' dies away with his death. Not how great he was, but what he was, engages our attention, and the searching demand that the soul of Robert Browning makes upon each and all of us who care for the higher life of our nation is, 'What I have done for England, say.'

The kingdom of poesy hath many mansions. That on whose portals Robert Browning's name is inscribed is distinguished from its neighbours both by its huge size and by its massive strength. The style is Gothic with a curious infusion of Italian Renaissance. Notice, before we enter, the quaint gargoyles that in part adorn, in part disfigure, every portion of the architecture that is susceptible of ornamentation. Gaining entrance with some difficulty—for the porter is somewhat gruff and scant of speech, giving but slight guidance to the visitor—we are at first struck by the obscurity that reigns in the interior, only lit up here and there by lurid splashes of splendour at spots which are in direct contact with the outer sunshine. But one's eyes soon get accustomed to the dim religious light, and if we have to strain our attention to catch the scheme of ornamentation, our satisfaction is the greater when we have caught it. The decoration is elaborate and masterly, but it almost always gives one the impression of being unfinished, owing to its over-elaboration. The subjects, again, are often on a grand scale, and often in the grand style, but many of them claim only to be quaint grotesques. The fertility of design is, however, extraordinary, and the mansion is abundantly spacious, each room and each cranny having its own individuality, marring somewhat the unity of design of the whole. Two or three of the tapestries strike us as of clearer outline and more finished design than the rest; one in particular in which the chief figure is a gaunt musician followed by a crowd of joyous children. Another, too, of three horsemen takes us, as it were, out into the open, and we seem to feel the air rush past us as they ride. But there is no need to complain of the atmosphere any where; the air is fresh and sweet throughout; no closeness, no clouds of incense or whiffs of stifling perfume offend the nostril. One suite of rooms entrances our attention by its original scheme of ornament. In each the same design, in itself somewhat repulsive, is repeated in mirrors of different shape, parabolic, elliptical, concave, and the rest, distorting the image in each case, but giving, on the whole, a curious impression of reality. Altogether we leave the mansion with a feeling of having seen one of the great masterpieces of poetic architecture, and with an abiding sense of the high achievement and higher aspirations of the master builder.

But enough of allegory, though the one we give may serve as well as another to suggest the total impression made by Browning's work. The extent of his achievements is the most striking quality. Seventeen volumes represent the poet's legacy to his countrymen. And what volumes! Crammed with thought, suffused with imagination, crowded with figures with life more **real** than half the people we meet, filled with suggestion, historic, ethical, artistic, and contemporary, they represent at least fifty volumes, if their full meaning were drawn out and displayed. Nor has this huge bulk been attained by harping on a limited set of themes. On the contrary, his topics are bewildering in their variety. The players in *Hamlet* had not a more varied *répertoire*. No one could ever guess what a new volume of Browning would contain—whether it would **be** sportive or melodramatic, speculative or soul-searching. And **the** range of treatment was as extensive as that of subject. He was not a great metrical artist, but he at least utilised the metrical themes open to the English poet, with the

exception only **of the more** recent importations from France, the *rondeau* and the rest.
His remarkable versatility is, **perhaps,** best
shown by the fact that his most popular **pro**
ductions were descriptive pieces of pure **action**
—the themes of Hamelin and Ghent—which
were outside his ordinary **range of interest,**
wide as that was.

' **My** stress **lay** on **the** incidents **in the**
' development **of a** soul; little else is **worth**
' study.' These words from the dedication to
the reprint **of** *Sordello*—itself **the key** to all
Browning's more serious side—sum up his
method. Spiritual dynamics, the influence of
soul on soul, this is what his mind fixes upon
amidst all the plexuses of things. **Not** action,
but character, and not character formed, but
in the forming—there is the staple of Browning's art. **And** in that direction his **power is**
unique in the world's literature. Comparisons
have been made with Shakespeare in this
regard, but here **the** superiority **is with**
Browning without **a doubt, and a** moment's
reflection will show why **it must be so.** The
business of the true dramatist is **with action—**
with character too, but character formed, and
only so far as action brings out **the** character
that is already there. The conditions of Shakespeare's art prevented him from dealing with
character formation, modification, elevation,

development, or degradation, to the extent
that Browning deals with them. Here, too,
is the secret of Browning's failure as a dramatist, for failure it was for a man of Browning's
calibre not to excel pre-eminently. Who
would not prefer to have *Colombe's Birthday* or
A Blot in the 'Scutcheon as a dramatic idyll?
And the reason is that the dramatic side of
these dramas—the action—is not the thing for
which the poet cares or makes his audience
care. Two acts of *Colombe* pass without any
action whatever. Browning had a quick eye
for a dramatic situation; he was dramatic in
that sense, if you will. But of the power of
connecting such situations together into one
organic whole, in which each should add force
to each—of this, the true dramatic power, he
had singularly little. Even *Pippa Passes* has,
with all its grace and effectiveness, no real
dramatic unity. Pippa passes through a series
of dramatic situations, and so strings them
together; but it is from the outside. Contrast the far more effective way in which a
poet of infinitely less poetic force, but yet of
keener dramatic instinct, M. François Coppée,
has dealt with a kindred theme in *Le Passant*.
No, Browning was no born dramatist, and was
wisely advised by his own instinct to turn to
'Dramatic Idyls' or 'Dramatis Personæ,' or in
other words, dramatic situations instead of
dramas.

This interest in characterisation **led him
to one of** the most original **of his** themes
—the self-portrayal of the **humbug,** religious
(Blougram), political (Schwangau), or social
(Sludge). These **are,** undoubtedly, *tours de
force* **of a** remarkable kind—so remarkable,
indeed, that they condemn themselves as unfit
topics **for** poetry. **To be** poetical **about the**
very antithesis **of poetry; to** present the hum-
bug and the materialist—and sympathetically,
for that is one of the conditions of **the** problem—in a medium which presupposes sin-
cerity and idealism as essentials,—such **was**
the task Browning set himself in these studies.
The failure was magnificent, **but it** was a
failure; the pieces are rhetoric, ingenious and
subtle rhetoric, not poetry **in** any sense of the
term that regards its essence as well as its form.
Akin to these studies **of** *problematische
Naturen*—'humours' **Ben** Jonson called **them**
—is **his** portrait-gallery of historical celebrities,
or rather obscurities, **his** *Parleyings with Certain
People of Importance in their Day,* a title **of**
one **of** his works that **would cover a large
section** of them. **It is characteristic of his**
method that his subjects are, **in almost** every
case, nonentities. No literary artist who **has
had** anything like his power of projecting him-
self into the past has refrained so rigidly from
dealing with **the** great **ones, the** successes **of**

history. His interest is with the failures ; why they failed, how often their seeming failure is the highest success, the battling of the brave but weak soul with the might of circumstance—these are the favourite themes of his historic imagination. Hence a somewhat exaggerated impression of the extent of his learning. By the very exigencies of the case his *dramatis personæ* had to be obscurities, and, owing to his intimate relations with Italy, these were mostly Italian obscurities, of whom Englishmen had no knowledge. Hence the impression, ' If he knows the obscurities so ' well, how well must he know the greater ' lights of history !' Put thus, one sees the *non sequitur.* He sought for the curiosities of history, and found them in volumes of memoirs, *causes célèbres*, and books like Wanley's *Wonders of the Little World.* He revived in this one of the favourite topics of the Middle Ages, the *Fall of Princes*, the *Mirror for Magistrates*, and his portraits recall the *exempla* of the mediæval moralists and sermonisers. In this again he was on the search for dramatic situations, and he was chiefly interested in the pathos of disappointment.

It is here that his spiritual influence has been most profound. No English poet has felt like Browning the pathos of the battle of life. Yet keenly as he felt it, he did not

despair nor bid the world despair. 'We bid
ye be of good hope' was his message to
the seeming failures in life, a class of ever-
growing importance in this self-conscious age.
His philosophy of life was eminently manly,
and has brought cheer to many a despairing
soul. If we could condense it into a formula,
the maxim would run, ' Aspiration is achieve-
' ment.' Herein his philosophy approached
closely one of the implicit assumptions of
the worldly life. The man of the world
regards every experience as such as a gain,
apart from its moral implications. It is better
to have sinned and lived than never to have
lived at all—never, that is, to have developed
one's own personality. Much of Browning's
thought comes perilously near this, and is
only redeemed from it by his acute sense of
the mordant poignancy of the conscience-pang.
On the whole, his influence is of the very
highest kind in this part of his work. It acts
as a moral tonic to be brought in contact with
such a manly, cheery soul, that does not faintly
trust the larger hope, but is confidently sure
that in aiming at the highest we are doing
the best for our best selves.

Nowhere is his influence higher in this
regard than in his love poems, the highest
test of a poet's powers. The world is right
in thinking that the chief business of the

poet is to express love and to teach how to love. Browning's love poems are equally remarkable for their range and for their intensity. Nowhere in English literature does this passion of love burn higher or burn purer. The passion that pulsates through *In a Balcony* or *In a Gondola* is as intense as anything in Heine, and yet it is purged of all fleshly dross. Not by any sacrifice of body to spirit, nor by any lapse into sickly sentimentalism, does Browning reach this result. The claims of the whole being, body and spirit, are admitted to the utmost, and as a consequence those of the former die away in the serener glow of the spiritual passion. As Browning regarding the struggle of life—the contest of soul with soul or against all souls—is eminently a man, so in his depicting of love—the union of soul with soul—he is pre-eminently the gentleman. Refinement is of the very soul of him, and that without, as so often happens, any loss of virile strength. Here more than anywhere we trace the influence of his marriage, that ideal union of two equally gifted souls which is unique in the world's history. How abiding was this influence was shown but a few months before his death in the Fitzgerald incident. It was clear enough to the dispassionate observer that Fitzgerald was speaking of Mrs. Browning the writer, not Mrs. Browning the woman. But Browning could be no dispassionate observer of the slightest aspersion on his wife, and in a spirit of almost boyish gallantry struck out on behalf of the wife who had been taken from his side more than a quarter of a century.

This is, perhaps, the place to treat of Browning's humour—a necessary side of a complete poetic nature, indeed of any complete man. Browning's gift in this direction was large, as witness the *Piper*, *The Two Poets of Croisic*, and the whole series of studies of humbugs and nonentities to which we have referred. But it is somewhat one-sided, allied to his interest in the pathetic, and thus somewhat grim. But it is never cynical, except when dealing with cynics; and though it is rarely hearty or a direct object of his art, it is always refined and manly. Mr. Ruskin, in a passage remarkable for its insight and for the quarter whence it comes, notices how inevitably the strongest English poetic force tends to degenerate into coarseness. Chaucer, Shakespeare, Dryden, Byron, are instances of what he means. Browning is the exception to the rule—he has the strength of these, but he has not their coarseness—and here again we probably have to thank the influence of the *Lyric Love* that interpenetrated his whole being during the greater part of his life.

All the qualities we have been noticing— his virile strength, his humour, his refinement, his interest in the pathetic, the pureness and intensity of his passion, his interest in the obscurities of history, his fertility and many-sidedness, his eye for the dramatic situation, but want of the true dramatic instinct—all these qualities culminate in *The Ring and the Book*, his greatest work in point of size and in the sense it gives us of his sustained power. But the whole impression is one of power misdirected. Not to speak of the irritating *bizarreries* of the advocates and of the fractions of Rome, the whole method of the book is anti-poetical. Poetic truth does not consist in displaying the facets of truth disconnectedly : the poet sees life singly and sees it whole, and should enable us so to see it. But if the experiment of trying to give the totality of truth by presenting its dislocated parts in small doses is a failure, what gigantic powers are displayed in the failure ! The Titan piles Pelion on Ossa, and if he fails to reach the all-commanding heights of Olympus, the massy pile remains as an enduring monument of his strength ; and the incidental successes on the way to the failure would be sufficient to found a dozen poetic

reputations. The contrast of Guido's two
soliloquies, Pompilia's purity, the Pope's placid
objectivity—these and a thousand other points
betray the master's hand. It has been said
that the whole concentrated energy of *Vanity
Fair* finds **a vent** through Colonel Crawley's
knuckles as he stretches the marquis at his
wife's feet. So the whole pathos and tragedy
of *The Ring* **and** *the* **Book** finds utterance **in**
Guido's **last words** :—

> Abate—Cardinal—Christ—Maria—God, . . .
> Pompilia, will you let them murder **me**?

but the highest order of poet—one that con-
trols his faculties instead of being controlled
by them—would not have been led astray
from such effects as these by over-refinements
of intellectual subtlety.

There we reach the last quality of Browning's mind **of** which **we** need take explicit
notice, and this intellectual subtlety is the
disturbing element in **his art.** He **is** both
too intellectual and too subtle. These are
qualities the reverse of poetical. Not that
a poet need be **a fool** or dense. But the
things of the intellect must be subordinate **to**
the purposes of his art, not objects of inde-
pendent interest. The intellect analyses and
abstracts, poetry synthesises and concretes.
In consequence of Browning's interest in **the**

gambollings of the human intellect, and especially of his own intellect, much of his work
reads like so many exercises in forensic dia-
lectics. 'What a grand Q.C. the world has
lost!' is our thought, but that is not a
thought that a great poet should arouse.
The Browningites, with the perverse ingenuity
of the uncritical worshipper, lay stress upon
this side of the poet's characteristics as if it
were his most desirable quality. 'He is
so subtle,' say they, and think they have
thereby pronounced his greatest praise. Profound a poet should be, but hardly subtle.
All art is at root selective; the poet's art consists in selecting out of the mass of thoughts
and feelings which a poetic subject arouses in
his soul those streams of thought and emotion
that are essential to the subject. But Browning too often did not select, but gave, or
attempted to give, the whole mass. The
outcome has its interest—the interest of the
riddle and the puzzle, which have their attraction for the uncultivated or the immature
mind. But it is a vital mistake to confuse
this interest, as the Browningites do, with the
poetic effect which the poet *quâ* poet alone
arrives at. 'How clever I am to have solved
that!' is the feeling produced by the solution of the riddle. We have no quarrel with
the feeling, but it is vastly different from the

proper ejaculation after being moved by the
poet, 'How noble to have felt that !'

Akin to this is the error of placing in the
forefront of his work the argumentative dis-
quisitions on theological subjects, which **form**
no inconsiderable portion of his poetical activity.   There is no reason why **a** poet should
not be **a** theologian ; **in these** days, which
have seen more theological disquisition than
any period since the Council of Trent, there
is every reason why a poet should share in
such an absorbing interest of the audience he
addresses.   But he has not to display the
processes of his thoughts on theology ; he **has**
only to give results in imaginative form.
Browning has shown how to do this in *Rabbi
ben Ezra*, but he has also shown us how not to
do it in *La Saisiaz*.   The poet may be—nay,
he must **be—very** sure of God and of an
eternal **soul, but he** is to convince us by his
very sureness, not by process of reasoning.

We have now touched **on** all **the** sides **of**
the poetic activity of Browning which need
touching upon for the purpose of indicating
the poetic force of the man, the large stores
of spiritual energy which are contained in
his works.   But poetry has form as well as
force, and we know but half of a poet's art
when we have measured his poetic force.
And **in** judging of Browning's poetic form

there can be no hesitation about the verdict. He was faulty in form almost always—fault-less scarcely ever. Often, indeed, his choice of metre struck a false note from the start; he wrote argument in jerky trochaics, he ex-pressed lyric emotion in blank verse. Such lapses in a man of sure touch in matters of this sort point to some inherent defect in the poet's method. Worse even than this was the over-subtlety of intellect to which we have already referred, and which is at the root of his so-called obscurity. He attempted not only to give the emotive iridescence of the poetic afflatus, but also at the same time to suggest the accompanying inrush of cluster-ing thoughts. The psychology of the poetic afflatus is obscure, but one thing is at least certain about it. Under the inrush of the emotive impulse the poet remains master of his passion, directing it into artistic channels. Browning had this power to the highest, and misused it. He attempted the impossible task of setting forth in verse the totality of impressions, emotional, æsthetic, and intel-lectual, which his object made upon him. When one reflects on what the totality of impressions on such a nature as Browning's must mean, one recognises the impossibility of the task. To make even an approach to it he had to write in a kind of lyric shorthand,

and his sentences become **congested with suggestion.** Hence their stimulating effect, **but it is not a** poetical one. **The poet's art** consists in selecting **one** particular **order of** impressions out of the totality which 'inspires' him. To attempt **to** give **the** whole **is, we** will not say inartistic, **but** extra-artistic. **The** poetic influence **is** diffracted and dispersed among **the** conflicting orders **of** interest that are aroused. **It** is much the same effect, to use **a** homely illustration, as **is produced** by the attempt **to** watch Barnum's five per-formances all at once. Only one art is capable of producing unity amid such com-plexity; not poetry, but music, was the art in which Browning's method was possible. His whole conception of poetic form was consequently false, and goes far to mar the greatest **poetic** force England has seen for centuries. Perhaps **the** secret of the matter was **that** his imagination **was** less intense than that of most **poets of anything like** his power. With them the **vivid** mental **picture** enables them to concentrate attention on **it, and** to inhibit, as the psychologists **say, the** crowd of surging thoughts that accompany it. **That** Browning had less of this visual insight **than** most poets is shown by the comparative **infrequency of** descriptive passages as well as **by a certain lack** of minute observation of externals. His insight was into the soul of things. His translations from the Greek brought out his imperfect form in a most instructive way. While he reproduced their spirit very effectually, he was hopelessly in-adequate in representing their form. It was as if Greek temples had been transformed into Gothic cathedrals. The sense of rugged power is always with us, rarely or never the impression of god-like grace. He was of the Titans, not of the Gods.

Standing by his open grave, we give the last thought to the man we have lost as well as the poet. His warm geniality made him a universal favourite in society. If to some it seems incongruous to think of the *vates sacer* at the five o'clock tea-table, it must be re-membered that the spiritual influence of such a nature would radiate through the very class that needs idealising. With him has gone a spiritual force of the first magnitude. The firm friend, the free giver, the sympathiser in all the higher forms of the nation's life, the inspirer of painting, music, and the higher criticism — all these are gone in Robert Browning the man. And notwithstanding all deductions of faulty form, of infelicitous choice of subject and medium, a large body of work remains of Browning the poet in which these imperfections were reduced to a minimum. **If** aspiration were indeed achievement, Robert Browning would **have** been the greatest name **in** the **roll** **of** English poets; **and** even **as** it **is,** his work **will** rank among the greatest spiritual forces **of** England.

JOHN HENRY NEWMAN

August 11, 1890

CARDINAL NEWMAN

GREAT leader **of men, an in-**fluential ecclesiastic, **a man of** saintly life, **a** spiritual force of great power, a master of English prose, has passed away from us with John Henry Newman. **To** modern England he has been as one of the dead from the night Father Dominic, the Passionist, passed over his threshold at Littlemore, and he has himself written the biography **of** that dead self in one of the masterpieces of English literature. What Father Newman did in life and letters is of quite subordinate interest to **the** spiritual career of the Fellow of Oriel, who exercised so **much** influence **on the** Church of **England and might have** exercised more. **It is only** so far as **that career has** affected **the** inner life **of** England **and** its manifestations in English letters that **it can be** considered in this place.

It seems almost a paradox to say of the **author of forty** volumes that his true sphere was in action, not thought or literature. Yet **it is a paradox** that contains more than the

119

usual fraction of truth.   He was born to lead
men ; the very modesty that caused him at
times to deny this concealed his dissatisfaction
even with the enormous mastery over men's
souls and fates that he wielded for so many
years.   It was by personal intercourse that he
sought to move the world, and did move it.
The tenacity with which he clung to old
friendships was significant of much.   His
whole life was a sermon, the text of which
might well be the title of his epoch-making
discourse, *Personal Intercourse the Means of Pro-
pagating the Truth*—the sermon that really
started the Tractarian Movement, and not
Keble's on National Apostasy.   Throughout
his Anglican period the ecclesiastical things
which touched him most nearly were not
things of dogma, but lay in the sphere of
almost practical politics.   At every point of
his career it was some problem in the relations of Church and State that affected him
most strongly.   The abolition of the Irish
bishoprics, the miserable muddle of the
Jerusalem bishopric, the alliance of O'Con-
nell and the Whigs—these things, and things
like these, are the turning-points of his
career.   Even the diplomatic reserve and
' economy of truth' with which the world
credited him for so many years were marks
of the ecclesiastical statesman, not of the
religious thinker.

It bears out this classification of him **as a man** of action, not of thought, that **almost** every one of the forty volumes of which we have spoken is what might be termed occasional. His sermons, fine as they are, **are occasional on the** face of them. 'Tract No. xc.' is **a** tract **for** immediate consumption. The magnificent *Apologia* is **but a** pamphlet writ large. **His** *Verses* are, as their title-page informs **us, 'on** Various Occasions.' Even when he engaged in works that might **seem** to imply a purely theoretic interest, like his *Essay on Development*, they were written with **a** practical aim, even though it were a personal one—of working the subject out to 'quiet him,' **as** he said, somewhat after **the** principle of κάθαρσις, familiar to the Greeks **and to** Goethe. His **was** not the writer's nature **that is** irresistibly impelled **to** writing and **thinking for their own** sakes. He thought, **he** wrote, **that he** might influence the actions of **men. He did** influence their actions, but, **as a consequence,** most **of** what he wrote has in reality died **away** with **its** practical effect, and of his forty volumes but a few sermons, 'Lead, kindly Light'—the one **hymn of** our language—the *Apologia*, and perhaps *The Idea of a University*, will form permanent additions **to** English literature. His histories **are** unhistorical, **his** criticism

uncritical, and much of his theology is founded
on his history and his criticism. His *Arians*
and his *Via Media,* his *Anglican Difficulties,*
even his *Grammar of Assent,* have mainly a
personal interest to commend them.

And yet what literary powers were those
that thus seem to have been squandered
away on temporary objects! Bizarre as his
reasoning seemed to most of us, how subtly
he weaved the weft of it! Dealing for the
most part with subjects remote from human
interest, he would so order his argument
that it would have the attraction of a plot
for us. Topics that seemed forbidding both
for their theological technicalities and their
repulse of reason were presented by him
with such skill that they appeared as inevitable as Euclid and as attractive as Plato.
All the resources of a master of English style
—except, perhaps, one, description—were at
his command; pure diction, clear arrange-
ment, irony, dignity, a copious command of
words combined with a reserve in the use of
them—all these qualities went to make up
the charm of Newman's style, the finest flower
that the earlier system of a purely classical
education has produced. It is curious, by the
way, that the only two men of our time who
have written on theology and possessed a
style, Dr. Martineau and Newman, have had

Huguenot blood in their veins. And with
Newman all this was informed with the
attraction of a personality so rare and a
nature so rich that the appeal is irresistible
even to those who care little for his topics.

Yes, that was an exceptionally rich nature
which has just been removed from the world.
He moved many men, because he had within
him the making of many men. He had
points of contact with nearly all the currents
of thought and feeling which were to transform the higher England in Queen Victoria's
reign. That revolt of his against ' Liberalism,'
as he called it, was prophetic of nearly all the
deeper movements of our time. The resort
to history for spiritual nourishment, which led
him from the Evangelicalism of Simeon to
Rome herself, has become a source of inspiration for the higher politics and economics of
our time. There was something, too, of the
romantic temper in him—that return to the
mystic glow and imaginative colouring of the
Middle Ages that has done so much for our
literature and our art. Even the method of
evolution appears to have operated on Newman's mind in the doctrine of development
that finally led him to Rome. And that
absorbing interest of Newman in dogmatic
theology was but a foreshadowing of what
has befallen most of England's higher minds

during the past half-century, even when it has led them to agnosticism. England is the only European country that cares for theology, say continental observers, and its passionate interest in theology begins in this century with the movement with which Newman's name will for ever be connected. Even the rise of the interest in art and music seems to be foreshadowed in Newman's own personal fondness for them. Newmanism, as we may call it, included all these things, and thus touched the national life in the early decades of Queen Victoria's reign in far more points than might seem at first sight to be the case.

But it was chiefly and mainly in his passion for theology that he came nearest to the higher strivings of his countrymen. In no one of his time was manifested more strongly the wish to believe which some of his disciples have ranked so high above the desire to know. His whole life was dominated by this wish, and it is this that gives such dramatic unity to the *Apologia*. No other autobiography—certainly not that of St. Augustine, its nearest prototype in literature—is so intensely theological. It is not the life of a man we read, it is the drama of a soul, and of a soul entirely occupied with the relations of itself to God. Surely few men have always lived their life so completely in the

great Taskmaster's eye. He seems to have
ever lived in the spirit of that childish fancy
of his, that the men around him were angels
disguised in human form—in other words,
that God and he were the only noumenal
realities of the world. It was characteristic
of his whole tone of thought that in dealing
with what seemed to be a purely logical
problem in his *Grammar of Assent*, he postulated
a new sense—the Illative Sense—clearly for ____
the one purpose of giving validity to faith.
Logician as he was, he subordinated here, as
elsewhere, the claims of logic to the claims of
theology.

What was it, then, that caused ' Newmanism' to be ultimately ineffective and led
Newman further and further away from the
main currents of English thought and feeling ?
All these rich forces of his spiritual nature
were tyrannised over by a subtle intellect
and a passion for logical consequence which
is furthest removed from English habits of
mind, and may, perhaps, be traced to his
Huguenot mother, as it has been equally ex-
emplified, though in an opposite direction,
by Professor Newman, the Cardinal's brother.
No Frenchman could be more consequent in
following logic to an absurdity than Newman.
Now English institutions, whether of State
or Church, are founded on compromise, or

the renunciation of logical consistency. Hence the aloofness of Newman from the practical course of English politics, ecclesiastical or constitutional. There is something foreign about his whole tone of thinking, which has found a natural and logical outcome in his death as a cardinal of the Roman Church. The same attitude of mind accounts for his deficiency in the essentially English feeling of humour, which is intimately connected with the spirit of compromise. Irony he possessed in all its efficacy, but the attempts at humour in his so-called novels, *Loss and Gain* and *Callista*, are strained in the extreme.

How comes it, then, that Newman, of all men in the world, with his hatred of compromise and thirst after logicality, should have ever thought to find rest in a *via media*, a compromise among compromises? There comes in another quality of his mind, which is equally un-English outside the particular profession for which it is appropriate. In reckoning up the formative influences on his character, something should be said of the legal tone which was given to it in early years by the fact that he was intended for the Bar. There is a curious touch of the man of the world in much that was done and said by the author of the *Dream of Gerontius*. In much of his dialectic there is a subtlety of distinction which recalls the legal quibble, and at times even the legal fiction. It was a crude feeling of this that caused Kingsley to ask his famous question, 'What, then, does Dr. Newman mean?' to which he obtained so crushing a reply. To the Philistine truth is a matter of yea or nay; there is no place for subtle gradations of meaning and reference. Kingsley was, with all his powers, something of a Philistine, and required this sharpness of outline in what we may term truths of the emotions. Newman easily overthrew the contention, but the very subtleties which he had to introduce into his defence, in all parts of it that were not merely personal, gave the British public an uneasy feeling that there was some justification for Kingsley's general position. Newman amply vindicated his own personal veracity, but he was scarcely so successful in removing all suspicion of what is euphemistically termed 'economy of truth' in the practice of the Church he had joined, and in his own method of dealing with theological problems. It was the *nisi prius* tone that left this impression, and it was generally this legal and quibbling tone in the treatment of religious topics that helped to undermine Newman's influence from the time of the appearance of ' Tract No. xc.'

It was, too, this *nisi prius* attitude that
enabled Newman to believe as long as he did
in his *via media*.   It is impossible even at this
distance of time to explain with any clearness
the subtle distinctions which in Newman's
mind differentiated the Anglican Church, as
the *via media,* from the Roman Catholic
Church.   The distinctions he makes are
exactly of the legal kind.   There was no
room in his mind for what Englishmen would
call the common-sense method of solving the
difficulties his own subtleties had raised.   He
never to the last faced the plain fact that the
Roman Catholic Church no longer occupies
the position of the Church of the fifth century
or of the fifteenth.   That Church is so far
removed from the tone and feeling of the
modern world that it is impossible to consider
conversion to its fold anything but *il gran
rifiuto* of these latter days—a renunciation of
all the privileges the modern mind holds dear ;
and, to do it justice, the Roman Church fully
recognises] the fact.   But it remains that
Newman did make the renunciation, and
thereby declared his antipathy to the modern
ideals.   They who hold to those ideals may
admire Newman, but they must condemn his
renunciation of reason and its claims.

He had the head of a lawyer, we have said,
but it should be added that he had the heart

of a saint.   The saintly life **has** never **been**
more faithfully followed than by John Henry
Newman.   **It is** due **to** his life more **than** to
his doctrines or his presentation of them that
so marked **a** change of public opinion **has**
occurred about Newman and about his Church.
After all, men judge creeds by the characters
they produce rather than by **the** logical **con-**
sistency **of their** doctrines.   That the pen-
dulum of public opinion about Roman Catholics
in England has swung back from violent
antipathy to sympathetic admiration **is due** in
large measure **to the saintly** life of John
Henry Newman.

HUTTON'S 'NEWMAN'*

R. HUTTON opens yet another new series by a biographical essay on Cardinal Newman, which seems likely to be the first of many biographies of the late Cardinal. It is but fair to Mr. Hutton to add at once that it was prepared during Newman's lifetime, and has not been hurriedly written to supply a demand caused by the Cardinal's death. It is far from a biography in the ordinary sense of the word ; of the man apart from the theologian we hear but little. Mr. Hutton has essayed to give a short history of Newman's religious opinions while he was in the Anglican Church, derived in the main from the *Apologia,* but told from a point of view necessarily less personal, and therefore more impartial.

In many ways the essay is successful in giving the reader the main critical points in that remarkable transition from the extreme left to the extreme right of Christian thought. Mr. Hutton's abstracts are clear, and his

* English Leaders of Religion.—Cardinal Newman. By R. H. Hutton. (Methuen & Co.)

criticisms judicious, if not profound. Yet somehow the total impression left is not a very decided one, owing, perhaps, to the absence of any summary of the main lines of development which led from Newman the Evangelical to Newman the Cardinal. The stages are clear, and have been discriminated once for all by Newman himself in the *Apologia*. It was difficult, if not impossible, for any one coming after Newman to improve on that statement, or amend it in any way. The chief merit Mr. Hutton's treatment can claim is that of conciseness.

The main lines of that development are familiar enough by this time to all who have read Newman's masterpiece. How the intense Evangelicalism of his boyish years was gradually dissolved and replaced by an equally intense conception of the authority of the Church, and how this led logically on to the momentous question, 'Which is the true Church?' how this was answered at first with the old high and dry Churchmen, and then, as the Erastianism of the Anglican Church as then constituted became clear, how the need of Church reform or reformation became apparent, and so the *via media* was devised as the ideal towards which the new reformation should travel—all this is something we have all known since 1864, if, indeed, it was not known earlier. Mr. Hutton has now and again a comment on the facts or the views, or he contests the contentions of the Tractarians on various points, but as a rule he tells again the twice-told tale, with clearness, indeed, but without much force.

It is only when he comes to the culminating episode—the composition of the *Essay on Development*—that Mr. Hutton offers much that is fresh or throws light on the matter in hand. The chapter devoted to this remarkable book is a closely written piece of analysis interwoven with comment that does credit to Mr. Hutton. He makes too much, perhaps, of the anticipation of Darwinism involved in such a treatment of doctrine. The idea was in the air at the time. Chambers's *Vestiges of Creation,* which appeared just then, was only the popularisation of much evolutionary speculation that was going on around Newman as he was writing his essay on the relation of doctrinal evolution and truth, for that is his main subject. What are the signs that show which doctrinal changes are development and which degeneration? That is the problem which Newman set himself to solve in the last year of his life as an Anglican. We all know the answer that he practically gave to the question, but it is of interest to have presented to us so clear a summary of the main points which led Newman to seek the true Church in Rome alone, and not, as heretofore, in the ideal Middle Way which he and his school were to make dominant in the Anglican Church.

The seven marks of true development were to be found in the Roman Church, and in the Roman Church alone, and therefore Newman joined that communion. The remarkable thing about all this is the intensely theological tone of the whole procedure—theological as opposed to religious. Mr. Hutton has a whole chapter devoted to a defence of Newman from the charge of being secretly infidel or sceptical. But to any one who reads a page of his writings it is abundantly clear that Newman never came within the region where doubt or infidelity exists. His whole attitude towards faith is a proof of this. He never needed a foundation for his faith, for the faith itself was a presumption in favour of the facts or feelings that were to prove the faith. This is perhaps not altogether a fair way of stating the case ; but Newman is consistent throughout in declaring that faith itself is the most effectual way of removing the difficulties that attend faith, nowadays most of all, but that have attended it at all times in the world's history.

Indeed, this utter absence of any scepticism

as to the fundamental principles of revealed
religion is implied in such a treatment of
theology as was adopted in Newman's writings both while he was within and after he
had left the Anglican Church. It is to him
the *scientia scientiarum*, a kind of deductive
science analogous to geometry, starting, like
it, with definitions, and assuming, like it, a
number of axioms. This conception at once
leads on to sacerdotalism, as it is obvious that
the knowledge of such a technical science and
its application to practice can only be safely
intrusted to experts. Hence the opposition
of the Tractarians to Protestantism, which from
this point of view represents the claim of
the common man to understand and apply
a highly technical science.

When we combine with this confidence in
the capacity of a dogmatic theology to solve
the difficulties of life an intense feeling of the
historic continuity of the race we have the
idées mères of Newman's position throughout
his career. The conception of the unity of
history is implied in all Newman's work, and
is the foundation of his conception of religious development that led him ultimately to
Rome. Simultaneously almost with Hegel's
philosophy of history Newman applied the
conception of evolution to man's spiritual
nature, before Spencer, Darwin, and Wallace

had applied the same ruling idea to organic nature. That this should have led him and his school to Rome is easily comprehensible now, but Newman's history in the Anglican Church was a bold attempt to claim for her the same privileges as the Church of Rome in this respect.

Mr. Hutton rests his claim for Newman's greatness on the persistency with which he applied himself to the working out in full detail of his main conceptions in theology, and on the greatness of the powers which, as Mr. Hutton intimates, he sacrificed to those objects. He might have been, it is argued, a great poet or a great literary artist in prose, and he gave this up in order to save the Church of England and to devote his whole energies to theology. It is very doubtful, we think, whether Newman would have become a great poet in any other way than he did, as a hymn-writer and as the author of *The Dream of Gerontius*. It is, again, somewhat difficult to guess in what direction but the theological Newman's exquisite prose, which at times became over-florid in his Romish works, could have been effective. He had few of the qualities that make the great historian, his literary essays are not even readable nowadays, and his so-called novels are only of interest in their theological bear-

ing.   Newman's whole mind and spiritual
feeling were against the whole position of
modern research—he could not bear not to
know.

Mr. Hutton is basing his hero's claim on
a false issue. Newman's claim to greatness
does not lie in any deliberate sacrifice of problematic powers for the sake of theological
science.   He deserves the name of great
because in an age of materialism and super-
ficial intellectualism he held aloft the banner
of spiritualism, because amidst all obloquy and
insult he held to what he considered the
truth, because he yielded up the proud position of a great spiritual leader to follow the
inward summons.   He has been one of the
operative forces that have aided to transform
England.   It is for this reason he has been
honoured and mourned by Englishmen of all
creeds, quite apart from the merits and demerits of the theology to which he devoted
his saintly life.

'LETTERS,' ETC.*

FTER a great man's death the floodgates of biography are opened. First come the press memoirs, often running to the length of monographs, then the magazine articles and the popular lives, and the climax is reached by the official biography; itself, perhaps, to be followed by rival lives, or at least popular summaries. This familiar process is clearly being followed in the case of Newman, and we are now in the midst of the first onrush of the waters. The three books under notice include the first instalment of the official biography, dealing with Newman's life as an Anglican, Mr. Fletcher's popular life, and a revised reprint of Mr. Meynell's excellent magazine articles. The two latter are written from a Roman Catholic point of view, the first from that of an Anglican, and thus

* *Letters and Correspondence of John Henry Newman.* Edited by Anne Mozley, 2 vols. (Longmans & Co.)

A Short Life of Cardinal Newman. By J. S. Fletcher. (Ward & Downey.)

John Henry Newman. By W. Meynell. (Kegan Paul & Co.)

137

together they cover the whole development of Newman's career.

It will always be impossible, as it will be unnecessary, to write or rewrite Newman's life as an Anglican. The *Apologia* stands in the way, in which he himself wrote his early life once and for all time. True, it is only the 'History of his Religious Opinions.' But with Newman, more, perhaps, than with any other man, his religious opinions were his life. Certainly Miss Mozley's work does not profess to retell the story of the *Apologia*. Her volumes are, in fact, a huge appendix to that work, containing the *pièces justificatives* for it. They are full of materials, but these do not explain themselves, and at every turn have reference to the events spoken of in the *Apologia*.

In large measure this supplement to Newman's religious autobiography is the work of Newman himself. He has throughout the two volumes edited the letters and added explanatory words and notes, which often read very oddly, interspersed as they are in the midst of the text. Indeed, it seems probable, from the date attached to many of these annotations,—1860,—that something like the present collection was intended to do the work that the *Apologia* itself did so efficiently. If that be so, the world owes a large debt of

gratitude to Kingsley for having provoked the
more artistic presentation of the facts. It
would be quite safe to prophesy, if one can
prophesy about past events, that Newman's
name would have far different associations with
it if these volumes, or volumes similar to them,
had taken the place of the *Apologia*. While
nearly every line of that masterpiece is of en-
trancing interest, there is scarcely a single page
in these two bulky volumes which anybody
would care to read again for its own sake.
Part of this unreadableness is due to the want
of explanatory and connecting matter. There
is not even a list of the celebrated Tracts.
The second volume in particular, which is entirely devoted to the 'Movement,' is in the main a
collection of business letters, the business being
of a highly ideal character no doubt, but still
its details are in large measure of the character
of machinery. Whether intentionally or no,
almost everything of human interest has been
eliminated from these pages, which are filled
throughout with controversial and theological
details, with scarcely any reference to the
feelings and aspirations of the workers in
the ' Movement.'

These volumes, then, must be regarded as a
supplement to the *Apologia*, and their direct
interest is the additional light they throw on
its pages. The main increase of knowledge

about Newman's life consists of an autobiographical memoir running to some seventy-
six pages, and bringing his life-history up to
the summer of 1832, the year preceding the
beginnings of the 'Movement.' This is, unfortunately, written in oblique narration, and
thus loses much of its vividness. Take, for
instance, the following passage :—

'The Provost's butler—to whom it fell by
' usage to take the news to the fortunate
' candidate—made his way to Mr. Newman's
' lodgings in Broad Street, and found him
' playing the violin. This in itself disconcerted
' the messenger, who did not associate such an
' accomplishment with a candidateship for the
' Oriel Common-Room ; but his perplexity was
' increased when, on his delivering what may
' be supposed to have been his usual form
' of speech on such occasions, that "he had,
' he feared, disagreeable news to announce, viz.
' that Mr. Newman was elected Fellow of Oriel,
' and that his immediate presence was re-
' quired there," the person addressed, thinking
' that such language savoured of impertinent
' familiarity, merely answered, "Very well,"
' and went on fiddling. This led the man to
' ask whether, perhaps, he had mistaken the
' rooms and gone to the wrong person, to
' which Mr. Newman replied that it was all
' right. But, as may be imagined, no sooner

' had the man left, than he flung down his
' instrument, and dashed downstairs with all
' speed to Oriel College. And he recollected,
' after fifty years, the eloquent faces and eager
' bows of the tradesmen and others whom he
' met on his way, who had heard the news,
' and well understood why he was crossing
' from St. Mary's to the lane opposite at so
' extraordinary a pace.'

If the reader will translate this back into
I's, my's, and *me's,* the gain of vividness will
be apparent. It is a pity that Miss Mozley did
not induce the Cardinal to reconsider his choice
of form for this autobiographical fragment.
The gain such a narration receives from being
put in the first person may be illustrated
by the following letter embedded in the
memoir :—

' On Wednesday, April 29, about breakfast-
' time, Mr. Wilson and Mr. Short called for
' me, and asked me whether I intended to
' stand for the scholarship. I answered that
' I intended next year. However, they
' wished me to stand this year, because they
' would wish to see me on the foundation. I
' said I would think of it. I wrote home that
' day. How often was my pen going to tell
' the secret ! but I determined to surprise you.
' I told you in a letter written in the midst of
' the examination that there were five [candi-

' dates] of our own [men]; did you suspect
' that I was one of the five? A Worcester man
' was very near getting it. They made me
' first do some verses; then Latin translation;
' then Latin theme; then chorus of Euripides;
' then an English theme; then some Plato;
' then some Lucretius; then some Xenophon;
' then some Livy. What is more distressing
' than suspense? At last I was called to the
' place where they had been voting; the Vice-
' Chancellor [the President] said some Latin
' over me; then made a speech. The electors
' then shook hands with me, and I immediately
' assumed the scholar's gown. First, as I was
' going out, before I had changed my gown,
' one of the candidates met me and wanted to
' know if it was decided. What was I to say?
' "It was." "And who has got it?" "Oh,
' an in-college man," I said; and I hurried
' away as fast as I could. On returning with
' my newly-earned gown, I met the whole set
' going to their respective homes. I did not
' know what to do; I held my eyes down. By
' this I am a scholar for nine years at £60 a
' year. In which time, if there be no Fellow
' of my county (among the Fellows), I may be
' elected Fellow, as a regular thing, for five
' years without taking orders.'

These four autobiographical chapters and
the accompanying inter-chapters in which Miss

Mozley **has given** supplementary documents
form the most important addition to our knowledge of Newman and his career contained in
these volumes.   They tell us of his early home
and education.   They give interesting details
like that **just** given of his college **career.**
Above all, they display him in a more secular
aspect, so **to** speak, than we are accustomed **to**
regard him.   **As he** himself informs us, it was
only on his election to the Oriel Fellowship
in 1822 that the possibility of a theological
career occurred to him.   Besides this they
give glimpses of the charming character of his
sister, Mary, whose loss affected him so deeply.
The fragments of her letters have a girlish
charm that lightens the somewhat gloomy and
austere tone of the book, so rarely relieved by
touches of humour from Newman or his correspondents, the only exceptions being Keble and
Hurrell Froude.

A large part of the first volume is taken up
by Newman's impressions during his grand
tour with the Froudes in 1832-33.   Much **of**
this is not of extraordinary interest, and might
have been well omitted.   Yet it is quite true
—and this is one of the main points brought
out in this work—that the solitary travel in
Sicily and the fever that overtook him there
formed the crisis in Newman's life.   His escape
from death might easily seem miraculous and

a special sign of grace to so ardent a believer. But for the untiring attention of his courier, Gennaro, his life would have paid the penalty of a somewhat hazardous exploit. His feeling of special mission was intensified by the narrow escape from death.

The celebrated hymn 'Lead, kindly Light,' turns out to be the exact expression of the deep feelings aroused by his Sicilian experience; it was written, as is well known, on his voyage to Marseilles during his convalescence. Almost every expression has a personal reference : 'I am far from home,' 'those angel faces' (his father and sister Mary), 'Pride ruled my will' referred to the strong feeling Newman had that his Sicilian illness was a punishment for his self-will. Even 'the moor and fen, crag and torrent,' were probably the reflex of the deep impression Sicilian scenery had made upon him. If one could generalise from a single example—and one often does so generalise in the first instance—it might seem that the popular effect of a poem depends on the intensity of personal feeling with which it is written. A poem's impressiveness, one might say, depends on the number of heart's drops instilled into it.

On this Sicilian illness there is a remarkable paper of Newman's in this volume which is almost morbid in the detail with which it

enters into each phase of the fever. Incident-
ally it contains a piece of self-portraiture, which
is perhaps, taking all things together, the most
striking thing in these volumes :—

'Indeed, this is how I look on myself; very
' much (as the illustration goes) as a pane of
' glass, which transmits heat, being cold itself.
' I have a vivid perception of the consequences
' of certain admitted principles, have a con-
' siderable intellectual capacity of drawing them
' out, have the refinement to admire them, and
' a rhetorical or histrionic power to represent
' them ; and, having no great (*i.e.* no vivid) love
' of this world, whether riches, honours, or
' anything else, and some firmness and natural
' dignity of character, take the profession of
' them upon me, as I might sing a tune which
' I liked—loving the Truth, but not possessing
' it, for I believe myself at heart to be nearly
' hollow, *i.e.* with little love, little self-denial.
' I believe I have some faith, that is all ; and,
' as to my sins, they need my possessing no
' little amount of faith to set against them and
' gain their remission. By-the-bye, this state-
' ment will account for it, how I can preach the
' Truth without thinking much of myself.'

It must be remembered that this was
written in a moment of self-depreciation, sincere enough, but rather tending to exaggerate
demerits and failings. But external evidence

and the general impression made by Newman
on his contemporaries show that these lines
are more truthful than such self-portraiture
usually is.   With regard to his coolness there
is a confirmatory passage in a letter in the
second volume, where he describes in an
amusing way his meeting Arnold—the chief
representative of 'Liberalism' in the Church
—in the Oriel Common-Room :—

'I was most absolutely cool, or rather calm
'and unconcerned, all through the meeting
'from beginning to end; but I don't know
'whether you have seen me enough in such
'situations to know (what I really believe is
'not any affectation at all on my part; I am
'not at all conscious of any such thing, though
'people would think it) that I seem, if you
'will let me say it, to *put on* a very simple,
'innocent, and modest manner.   I sometimes
'laugh at myself, and at the absurdities which
'result from it; but really I cannot help it,
'and I really do believe it to be genuine.   On
'one occasion in the course of our conversation
'I actually blushed high at some mistake I
'made, and yet on the whole I am quite
'collected.   Now, are you not amused at all
'this? or ought not I to blush now?   I never
'said a word of all this about myself to any
'one in my life before; though, perhaps, that
'does not mend the matter that I should say
'it now.'

Both passages concur in giving an impression of cool dispassionateness that contrasts with some of the impassioned language he used in self-defence against Kingsley and in his newspaper letters. Both Mr. Fletcher and Mr. Meynell remark that this passion was simulated and calculated on the part of Newman, who defended it on the plausible ground that the British public will never believe a man is in earnest unless he loses, or seems to lose, his temper.

The end of the first volume and the whole of the second are entirely taken up with letters and documents relating to the 'Movement' which gave new life to the Anglican Church, and led the leader of it to the Roman fold. It clearly forms the raw material—the very raw material—out of which Newman drew up his own lucid account, and it affords explicit information on every phase and divagation of Tractarianism in its formative period. But its very minuteness renders it practically unreadable; there is little or no connecting narrative—only a few 'Chronological Notes' of Newman's which assume in the reader a minute acquaintance with every turn of events in the long struggle. It thus affords a mine of evidence for the Oxford Movement, but its riches have to be dug for, and it is only to be used as a supplement to the *Apologia* or to a book like that of Dean Church.

That these documents should confirm the *Apologia* is comprehensible enough, for they were mostly in Newman's hands when he wrote it, and have practically been edited by him before now being given to the world. Here and there we catch a glimpse of editorial motive : thus the note on vol. i. p. 476, 'First mention of Pusey's name,' and the entries from Newman's *Journal*, vol. ii. p. 24, giving details of Pusey's movements, were clearly intended to dissociate Pusey's name from the ' Movement.'   Yet it remains to be proved whether the impetus and force given to it by Pusey's social position were not vital to the development of the ' Movement.'   As Mr. Meynell points out, it was Newman's family connections, or rather want of them, that threw the direction of the ' Movement ' into Pusey's hands, and gave rise to the popular epithet ' Puseyite.'   These are, however, almost the only instances of pettiness to be observed in these volumes, unless the reference to Golightly, vol. i. p. 165 (' he is better to know than to see '), can be regarded as such.   But the intense minuteness in personal details shows an amount of self-will and self-opinion in Newman which is extraordinary in a man of such genuine modesty.

The total impression given by the details of the ' Movement ' confirms the general idea

that has long been current. It was an
attempt to transfer the seriousness of Evangelicalism to the side of the High Church.
In a significant passage (vol. i. p. 277) Golightly declared that the only young men in
whom there was true seriousness were Calvinistic in tone. Newman had been trained
Calvinistically, and was thus adapted by his
training to make the required transition from
the Low to the High Church. As early as
1830 T. Mozley recognised his suitability as
leader of such a movement. Theologically
and technically speaking, Newman and his
followers made earnest, as the Germans say,
with the conception of the Apostolical Succes-
sion and all that it implies : 'Apostolical,'
indeed, becomes a cant word in these letters to
indicate the aims of the party. Newman was
thus, in Heine's phrase, though not in Heine's
sense, a Knight of the Holy Ghost, and
valiantly he fought the fight of the Faith.

Towards the end of the second volume
Newman's development had reached a stage
when Rome loomed in the distance as the
inevitable goal of his theological thinking.
It will come as a surprise to most people
that this stage was reached much earlier
than the final step would lead one to imagine.
At first, indeed, he was unconscious of the
direction of his steps; he did not know where

he was leading his followers, because he did not know how far he was going himself. So far he could honestly deny the imputation that he was a Romanist in disguise while seemingly fighting for a *via media* between Anglicanism and Romanism. But it appears from a touching series of letters between his sister and himself that he was practically a Romanist in disguise for some years—probably as many as four—before he took the final step. It is curious that his consciousness of being drawn towards Rome should have coincided in point of time with the rejection by the Anglican Church, and to a certain extent by his own party, of the doctrines of 'Tract No. xc.' Here again we seem to have glimpses of quasi-personal motives in what appear to be doctrinal developments that clash with our preconceived notions of his humility and disinterestedness in the highest sense of the word.

There is one thing that comes out in these letters that is explanatory of much. He was a theologian, or rather a theological thinker, but he was not, comparatively speaking, a theological scholar in the sense in which we can apply that term to Döllinger or even to Pusey. It is curious to find a thinker who laid such absolute stress on authority in the living Church, and on development in the

Church of the past, knowing so little about
the actual facts of that development. Historical criticism in the field of theology was
not born in his time, above all in England,
and there is an utter absence of any appeal
to it in these volumes.

Altogether these letters do not impress one
with very high ideas of the intellect of the
Tractarians. They all seem too deeply im-
mersed in the practical details of their schemes.
There is scarcely any discussion of principles,
or even any distinct consciousness of the
principles to be fought for. Resistance to
' Liberalism ' in its inroads on the Church is
a more prominent motive, it would seem,
than any distinct conception of the ideals
which they desired to realise. Even in
Newman there is too much immersion in
detail, and there is far too little of humanism
in his letters to make them interesting. It
is the 'Movement,' the 'Movement,' and
still again the 'Movement.' Of life, of art,
except stray references to music, of letters,
there is scarcely anything throughout these
thousand pages. It is possible that this was
designed by the editor and by the Cardinal,
but the result has been to make these volumes
terribly technical and monotonous.

The two remaining books on our list deal
more fully with the Cardinal's Catholic life.

In one way this was a failure, his Cardinal-deaconship being a somewhat empty honour, and he never acquired any real influence in his adopted Church, such as has been wielded by the rival English Cardinal. It is, indeed, curious to reflect that Newman's theological thoughts on the necessary development of religious truth should have led him into the fold of the Church which practically negatives the possibility of such development. There is clearly no field in her economy for the theological thinker; the Pope's infallibility renders such efforts nugatory. On the other hand, it must be remembered that the late Cardinal's work as a literary artist was mainly performed in his Catholic period. His novels, the *Dream of Gerontius*, the *Idea of a University*, the *Grammar of Assent*, even the *Apologia* itself, were all products of his Catholic period. Except the *Lyra* and the sermons—but what an exception is there!—the chief works by which he will be remembered were written within the Church of his adoption. And his life in that Church, when it comes to be told, must surely be more full of human and natural interest than the somewhat morbid and gloomy period that closed in 1845.

www.ingramcontent.com/pod-product-compliance
Lightning Source LLC
Chambersburg PA
CBHW020228030726
47497CB00009B/2996